THE

WANDERING JEW
HAS ARRIVED

ALBERT LONDRES

Translated from the French by Helga Abraham

gefen
publishing house בית הוצאה לאור גפן
JERUSALEM ◆ NEW YORK   Est. 1981

All biblical translations are taken from *The Holy Scriptures of the Old Testament: Hebrew and English*, © British and Foreign Bible Society, 1961.

Cover Design: Dragan Bilic – Pixel Droid Design Studio
Typesetting: Optume Technologies

ISBN: 978-965-229-889-8

3 5 7 9 8 6 4 2

Gefen Publishing House Ltd.
6 Hatzvi Street
Jerusalem 94386, Israel
orders@gefenpublishing.com
972-2-538-0247

Gefen Books
11 Edison Place
Springfield, NJ 07081
orders@gefenpublishing.com
516-593-1234

www.gefenpublishing.com
Printed in Israel

Library of Congress Cataloging-in-Publication Data

Names: Londres, Albert, -1932, author. | Abraham, Helga, translator.
Title: The wandering Jew has arrived / by Albert Londres ; translated by Helga Abraham.
Other titles: Juif errant est arrive. English
Description: Springfield, NJ : Gefen Publishing House, 2017.
Identifiers: LCCN 2016032286 | ISBN 9789652298898
Subjects: LCSH: Jews--Europe, Eastern--Social conditions. | Europe, Eastern--Social conditions. | Zionism. | Palestine--Description and travel. | Londres, Albert, -1932.
Classification: LCC DS135.E83 L6413 2017 | DDC 305.892/4047--dc23 LC record available at https://lccn.loc.gov/2016032286

Contents

Introduction

Has the Wandering Jew Arrived?
By Rav Daniel Epstein
Translated from the French by Helga Abraham

The Wandering Jew Has Arrived is a book like no other. Innumerable works have been written on the tribulations of the Jewish people across the world since Abraham was commanded by the divine voice to "Get thee out of thy country, and from thy kindred, and from thy father's house, unto a land that I will show thee" (Genesis 12:1) until the beginning of the twentieth century – innumerable books written by historians, theologians, writers and travelers. From their earliest days, the Jewish people left no observer indifferent. Each book throws light on another facet of a destiny rich in teachings and fraught with catastrophe. And yet Albert Londres's contribution to this infinite corpus cannot but move us. Reading it in 2017, we are caught between tears and laughter, between compassion for a world that was annihilated by the Nazi barbarity and worry for the future of the Jewish people ingathered in Zion.

Who was Albert Londres that he so ably understood the torments and hopes of the Jewish people? Born in 1884 and rising rapidly to the rank of international reporter, he became a unique witness to the precarious and often horrendous condition of the Jewish communities of eastern Europe on the eve of the Holocaust, as well as to the construction of the future State of Israel in Palestine. More than a journalist who recounted events, Londres was, throughout his career, a passionate chronicler of human suffering and a campaigner against injustice and cruelty. He was not content with reporting facts: he sought to rouse the conscience of his readers and call them to fulfill their responsibilities.

The first article with his byline described the German bombardment of Reims Cathedral and already bore the hallmark of his journalistic philosophy: "Our profession is not to give pleasure, nor to do harm; it is to twist the pen into the wound." Wounds were never lacking. His report on the penal colony of Cayenne ultimately led to the closure of this infernal institution, which he termed "a factory of evil." On his return from the Soviet Union, he denounced the "brainwashing drummed in by paid hacks." In Buenos Aires, he followed the traces of young Jewish women enticed from their homes in eastern Europe by the promise of rich marriages and forced into prostitution; in Africa, he described the ordeals of black workers; in mental asylums the cruelties inflicted on residents. Across the world, he scoured sites of suffering indefatigably, pen in hand like a weapon.

It is this interest in everything human and his sense of responsibility to chronicle the wounds in the flesh and soul of martyred humanity that led Londres, one day in 1929, to follow on the heels of a rabbi who had arrived in England from Galicia to raise funds for the survival of his community. This was to be the beginning of a journey that took him, stage by stage, to the far reaches of eastern Europe. He returned with unforgettable descriptions of the lives of Jews, observant and secular, Zionist and anti-Zionist, wonder rabbis, Hassidic *tzaddikim* and Lithuanian Torah scholars, an entire exotic world for this non-Jewish Parisian reporter with an insatiable curiosity. The ignorance proclaimed by Londres at the outset transformed his investigation into a voyage of initiation into the world of the Jews, a true terra incognita which he learned to decipher with the aid of a Zionist guide and unbeliever who served as his interpreter. In this way, he succeeded in enabling readers as ignorant as himself, and often deeply anti-Semitic, to share his discoveries and his neophyte enthusiasm.

How does one describe to a French public, nurtured for centuries on a "teaching of contempt"* and anti-Semitic clichés, the spiritual life of students of the Talmud in a Warsaw yeshiva? What would his readers make of this love of ancient texts so disparaged in Christian Europe and burned more than once in public places? Londres does not indulge in an erudite demonstration of the wisdom of the rabbis: he feigns derision and even revulsion for the smell of "essence of salted herring and essence of caftan fumes" that reigns over the "rabbi factory" and then immediately rebukes his prejudices…and those of his readers:

> How trivial my thoughts are! What does smell have to do with this place? The five senses and even the others never penetrated a *mesivta*. Nothing from outside has an impact on these students. Absolutely nothing! They are not here to eat, sleep, touch, hear, see, taste or feel, but to learn. The passion for learning is uniquely Jewish.

This passion for learning – in spite of cold, hunger, fatigue and a virulent anti-Semitism that often took the form of bloody pogroms – is

---

* Jules Isaac, *The Teaching of Contempt: Christian Roots of Anti-Semitism* (New York: Holt, Rinehart and Winston, 1964).

undoubtedly the real mystery of Israel and the secret of its survival in the Diaspora. But this ignorance about the outside world was not without risk: it prevented the Jews from understanding the gravity of the danger that threatened, in 1929, a helpless Jewish people amid hostile populations. The Jew, wrote Londres, is guilty of one crime: that of being Jewish. Which, of course, explains nothing. "Why these pogroms?" he asks:

> Why did the Turks kill the Armenians? Why does a cat scratch the eyes out of a dog? Because race speaks louder than humanity. A Hebrew always sticks in the throat of a Slav. And a long life together has not brought them closer. A Pole or a Russian chases a Jew from a pavement as though the Jew, who is passing by, is stealing his air. A Jew, in the eyes of an eastern European, is the incarnation of a parasite.

It is useless to look for the cause of hatred: "The fundamental cause of pogroms is loathing of Jews. Then come the pretexts."

In the alleyways of the ghetto, the Jews nurtured themselves on dreams. Londres is hosted at the Shabbat table of a family that has just suffered a pogrom:

> Everyone seemed very joyful. The concern for their safety temporarily lay dormant in the hearts of these souls, grouped, that night, at the foot of the throne of the Eternal, their King. When the cakes arrived, the father launched into a melody, one of those Oriental chants that tug at one's heart like a departing ship.

Another dream saves the Jews from despair: it is, of course, the Zionist dream. So Londres sets out for Palestine in order to watch the fulfillment of this dream and the return of the Wandering Jew to the land of his ancestors.

He witnesses a metamorphosis: the cowering Jew of the ghetto now holds his head high. Henceforth, he "could stand at his window and shout, 'I am a Jew! This is my glory!' without risking being tied on the spot to the tail of a wild mare. Open your eyes, the dream will not unravel – it is cemented in Tel Aviv!"

Londres marvels at the brand new Hill of Spring (Tel Aviv): "It is bright, spacious, sunny and all white. It is gay. It emanates a fierce determination to leave the ghetto behind." And the Hebrew language has "emerged from the tomb of the Talmud.... It is in Hebrew that a child calls his mother, that a lover lies to his beloved, and that neon signs entice passersby." But more surprises lie in wait for our indefatigable traveler: he finds the Wandering Jew in Jerusalem, praying at the Wailing Wall. When one of the faithful buries his head in his right hand, our Parisian feels like asking: "What's wrong, my fellow? Can I help you?" Even in front of the Wailing Wall, our explorer does not lose his sense of humor…

The Jews have returned to their land and found their pride again but, as in the time of Abraham, the land is inhabited and the Arab inhabitants react with violence at the return of the dispersed Jews. Pogroms recur, this time in Hebron; violence follows violence, but amidst the bloodbath, Londres detects sparks of humanity that offer a glimpse of hope against a backdrop of darkness: some Arabs "offer the shelter of their roofs to the future victims. One, a friend of a rabbi, even walks all night to pitch himself in front of the house of his protégé. He guards the entrance against the madmen of his own race."

Throughout the book, Londres's sympathy for the Jewish people in its exile and in its regained homeland does not cloud his perception of the future. Two peoples descended from Abraham claim the same Land. Will they be able to live in peace? It is only on this condition, which still appears distant, that one will be able to say: the Wandering Jew has arrived and, with him, all the wanderers of the earth.

We would like to conclude with this dream, but the last word belongs to our traveler to the Land of dreams. He is in Tel Aviv on the Jewish New Year, Rosh Hashanah.

> At the edge of the water, the Jews were acting very strangely. They seemed to be delving into their pockets in order to find something to throw. Then, they extended their arms in the direction of the Mediterranean: they were casting their sins into the sea!
>
> "It is about time!" I said to myself. "They have finally understood. As long as they do not forget to drown their excess pride, everything will end well."
>
> Is this a prophecy?
>
> Has the Wandering Jew arrived?
>
> Why not?

The question remains open....
Jerusalem, Shvat 5617/February 2017

Rav Daniel Epstein *has rabbinic ordination from the Harry Fischel Institute for Talmudic Research and an MA from the University of Strasbourg, France. He teaches at the Matan Institute and Midreshet Lindenbaum in Jerusalem, and at Tel Aviv University's Institute of Psychoanalysis.*

Preface

> Our profession is not to give pleasure, nor to do harm; it
> is to twist the pen into the wound.
>
> Albert Londres, *Terre d'ébène : la traite des noirs*
> (The land of ebony: The black slave trade)

Le Juif errant est arrivé (*The Wandering Jew Has Arrived*) by French journalist Albert Londres was published in France in 1930 and represents his most enduring work.

As one of the top journalists of his day, Londres could choose the stories and places *he* wanted to cover. After reporting on wars, conflicts and revolutions and taking up causes that ranged from French penal colonies to lunatic asylums, he decided to investigate the lives of Jews. A brief visit to Poland in 1926 had exposed him to the realities of pogroms and ghettos, and he wanted to know more about the "Jewish condition" and the context that propelled Jewish emigration to Palestine.

Thus, in 1929 he set off on an investigative journey that took him from Whitechapel to Prague, Subcarpathian Russia, Bessarabia, Bukovina, Lwow, Warsaw and finally Palestine. He entitled the series of articles he authored for *Le Petit Parisien* "The Drama of the Jewish People: From the Ghettos of Europe to the Promised Land,"

and subsequently polished this material to produce what is considered to be his literary masterpiece: *The Wandering Jew Has Arrived*.

Still widely read in France, the book came to my attention when the Hebrew translation was published in 2008 (Nahar Books). Surprisingly, I discovered that no English translation was available. An English translation had been published in 1932 but soon went out of print. I use the word *surprisingly* because it is hard to read this work without being arrested by its enormous significance – as a unique eyewitness account by a non-Jew of a pivotal period in Jewish history, as a major literary work in itself and as a masterful example of journalism at its best.

Londres's biographer Pierre Assouline describes his subject as "a poet of immediate history."* In his youth, Londres indeed aspired to a poet's life and published several collections of poems before devoting himself to journalism. Although he abandoned literary aspirations, he remained a poet at heart and it is this "poetic" dimension – his economy of words, graphic style, unforgettable metaphors, irony, wit and humor – that elevates his articles into works of literature. In one of the most striking chapters in *The Wandering Jew Has Arrived*, Londres outlines the birth of the modern pogrom. He lists the bare statistics – 150,000 victims, 300,000, one million – then pummels the reader with the horrific details. But it is his metaphors that remain etched in our memory: the pogrom as a specter that coolly strolls around eastern Europe terrifying Jews, the pogrom as a form of rabies that infects men and impels the rabid to bite only Jews. Elsewhere he offers vivid descriptions of the moods,

---

*   Pierre Assouline, *Albert Londres: Vie et mort d'un grand reporter, 1884–1932* [Albert Londres: Life and death of an international reporter, 1884–1932] (Paris: Balland, 1989), 17. All quotations from Assouline's work are my own translation.

smells, customs and wonderful personalities that characterized the
Orthodox world. In a rabbinical seminary in Warsaw, where he witnesses Torah-intoxicated students studying sixteen hours a day, he
notes astutely that not all of them will become rabbis when they
leave – but all of them will take up the profession of son-in-law!

In this short book, Londres covers a broad array of subjects:
the origins of Judaism, the daily lives of Jews, their well-honed
survival skills, their love of the Torah, the nature of pogroms, the
birth of Zionism, the anti-Zionist rabbis, the emergence of the
"new Jew" in Palestine and the virulent animosity of the local
Arabs. It is clear, in every line, that Londres was a journalist who
did his homework. His knowledge was astounding, his grasp formidable. Having done his homework, he was able to distill the
essence from the mass, distinguish truth from fiction and, being
a thinking man, confront his interlocutors with the implications
of their actions. Toward the end of the book, Londres recounts
a conversation he had with Ragheb Bey al-Nashashibi, the Arab
mayor of Jerusalem, during which the latter vowed there would
be more bloodshed against the Jews once the British left Palestine.
Londres responded:

"You can't kill all the Jews. They number one hundred
fifty thousand. It would take too long!"

"No," he said in a very soft voice. "Just two days!"

"Seventy-five thousand per day?"

"No problem!"

Presciently, Londres told the Arabs that they overestimated their
strength and that the "new Jews" would not let themselves "bleed
to death" but would pay them back in kind. His depiction of the
rabid anti-Semitism in Europe also seems to anticipate the horrors
of the Holocaust that would sweep across Europe just a decade after

the publication of his book, annihilating many of the communities he describes.

As for the modern State of Israel, it would be fascinating to imagine what Londres would have to say were he to fast-forward in time. He certainly could never have believed that the "old" Jewish world that he documented, with its prestigious yeshivas and learned rabbis, would resurrect itself in Israel, within a couple of generations, after having been decimated in Europe. In 1929, when he came to Palestine, he thought that the caftans, beards, sidelocks, fur hats and women's wigs of old were already relics of the past. How amazed he would be to see them "bobbing up" in every part of Israel and a flourishing ultra-Orthodox population numbering in the hundreds of thousands.

What Londres did get right was his sense that the fledgling Jewish state was being built on solid foundations and that the zeal and pride of the pioneers would see them through the hostilities that awaited them. "The new Promised Land," as he called it, held out hope for the persecuted Jews of Europe and, yes, he mused, perhaps it could be said that the Wandering Jew had finally come home.

I believe that anyone interested in Jewish history, the Israeli-Palestinian conflict and documentary literature per se will find Londres's book compelling and insightful. On a par with works of other great documentarians such as Mark Twain and George Orwell, *The Wandering Jew Has Arrived* is a timeless book that sheds a highly personal and original light on the "Jewish story," past and present.

On a technical note, as a translator, I strove to stay as true as possible to Londres's idiosyncratic style, metaphoric language and frequent changes of verb tense.

My two editors at Gefen Publishing House, Kezia Raffel Pride and Tziporah Levine, provided great professional expertise, helping to correctly render historical references, religious allusions, place names and linguistic terms.

Please note that parenthetical and bracketed insertions in the text are Londres's own. Editorial insertions added to the English translation appear in footnotes.

Helga Abraham
Jerusalem
Spring 2017

Acknowledgments

I wish to thank first and foremost Zohar Trifon, who brought *The Wandering Jew Has Arrived* to my attention and suggested I translate it into English. Zohar read the book when it came out in Hebrew in 2008 and immediately recognized it as a work of art that deserved to be made accessible to English-speaking readers.

Raphael Brenner encouraged and supported me all along the way, never doubting my abilities or the importance of the project. Raphael also served as my French language consultant, helping me to understand Londres's idiosyncratic modes of expression.

Susie Cohen, with her broad knowledge of Judaism and eastern European history, provided invaluable guidance on the correct rendition of the many geographic, historical and religious terms that abound in the book.

A special thanks also to Baruch Sirota for his expert linguistic guidance and patience.

Finally, I would like to dedicate this translation to the memory of my good friend Joan Hillel. An avid book lover and fervent Zionist, Joan appreciated the unique contribution of Londres's work to the historical record. Her steadfast moral support was invaluable.

CHAPTER 1

A Bizarre Personage

The boats that sail from Calais to Dover are called ferries. At the beginning of this year, the nineteen hundred twenty-ninth of the Christian era, I was on one of those ferries.

It seemed quite well built and order reigned on board. In the lowest compartment, travelers, standing in a long line, clutching passports, waited to present themselves to the police. Others, at the stroke of five o'clock, religiously made their way to the ritual rendezvous of the teapot. The staircase was crammed with worried souls. What was the sea plotting? Would they have to descend to the depths of the ferry? Or settle on its top? The top won; the crowd surged onto the deck.

There, a grand parade of suitcases was lined up!

The boat, which had been mute till now, began to speak.

Through the magic of their labels, the suitcases recounted their voyages. Scheherazade would not have been less eloquent. A snap of the Parthenon recounted that this one hailed from Athens. It had made a stop at a luxury hotel in Rome and then at an *albergo* in Florence. Another one looked indecisive: Had it not changed hotels three times in Cairo? A tiny one hailed from Brisbane with a stopover in Colombo. Several came from India. The pictures of the hotels of Bombay were much prettier than those of Calcutta. In a corner, a sorrowful one looked back nostalgically at Biskra, a palm tree glued on its side. A score came from Menton and Saint-Raphael. Switzerland too. On handsome leather, the snow and sun of other countries melancholically traversed the strait.

Suddenly, as I was thinking about all those folded, itinerant dinner jackets returning home to England, a bizarre personage loomed amid this luggage.

There was nothing white about him except his socks – everything else was solid black. His felt hat, which in better times must have been hard, was now somewhat limp. Nonetheless, this headgear represented the sole European feature of his wardrobe. A long, unbuttoned frock coat, which served as an overcoat, offered a glimpse of a second, greenish frock coat tied at the waist with a threadbare cord. This individual had a flowing beard, but the highpoint were the two locks of hair that escaped from his outlandish hat and hung, neatly curled, in front of his ears.

The English, being champions of the razor, looked at him with alarm while he strode up and down, above the melee.

This was a Jew.

Where did he come from? A ghetto.* He was part of those millions of individuals who still live under the Law dictated by Moses from atop Mount Sinai. To clarify things, one should add that, at the present time, they also live in Galicia, Bukovina, Bessarabia, Transylvania, Ukraine and the Marmarosh Mountains. In other words, without ceasing to belong solely to God, they are, as a result of man's will, Polish, Romanian, Russian, Hungarian and Czech subjects.

---

*   Londres uses the word *ghetto* to signify an eastern European shtetl, or Jewish neighborhood.

The man's outfit could have been his passport. He most probably came from Galicia, was certainly a rabbi and, as for the purpose of his journey, since we are acquainted with certain aspects of the lives of these Jews, this fact could easily be determined: the rabbi was on his way to London to collect *chalukah* (charitable funds).

The ferry did not tarry before unloading its content onto Dover quay. I stuck closely behind the holy man. Holding a polished wooden case, he followed the crowd. A policeman with a crested helmet smiled as he passed by. We quickly arrived in front of the customs counter. The rabbi placed his case on it. At that moment, and for the first time in my life, my heart quivered like that of a customs officer. Why were they taking so long before instructing him to unload his merchandise? Finally, they asked him to do so. The case revealed its secrets. A white shawl with black stripes and a fringe, a pair of socks, two small boxes slightly longer than matchboxes but twice as thick and tied to a leather strap, two big books which, from afar, smelled of the Talmud and a few newspapers printed in strange characters.

Prior incursions into the synagogues of eastern Europe enabled me to recognize that the shawl was a prayer shawl, a *tallit*, and the boxes were *tefillin*, which every pious Jew ties on his forehead and left wrist* when engaging in holy discourse with the Lord.

A Protestant customs officer could not be expected to understand the holiness of these objects – he handled them as though he were handling snuffboxes and a Spanish shawl. The baggage check completed, the rabbi made his way to the railway platform.

He let the Pullman pass by and, ten minutes later, caught the train of sensible folk.

---

* The *tefillin* (phylacteries) are worn on the left forearm (unless the wearer is left-handed, in which case the *tefillin* are worn on the right forearm).

Naturally, I chose a seat facing him.

My behavior was not dictated by whim. This man had arrived at exactly the right time in my life. I had set out this time not on a journey around the world, but on a journey around Jews, and I was going to tip my hat first in Whitechapel.

I would see Prague, Mukachevo, Oradea-Mare, Kishinev, Cernauti, Lemberg, Cracow, Warsaw, Vilna, Lodz, Egypt and Palestine, the past and the present, traveling from the Carpathians to the Mount of Olives, from the Vistula to the Sea of Galilee, from sorcerer rabbis to the mayor of Tel Aviv, from thirty-six degrees below zero, which the newspapers in Czechoslovakia were already heralding, to the sun which, every year in May, awaits those who sail into the ports of the Levant.

But I had to begin in London.

Why?

Because England, eleven years ago, had proclaimed to the Jews the same words that God, sometime before, had proclaimed to Moses on Mount Horeb: "I have resolved to deliver you from the oppression of Egypt and take you through the kingdoms of the Canaanites, the Hittites, the Amorites, the Perizzites, the Hivites and the Jebusites, to a land where the rivers flow with milk and honey."*

Lord Balfour expressed himself less poetically. He proclaimed to the Jews: *England, touched by your distress and anxious not to let another great nation settle on one of the banks of the Suez Canal, has decided to send you to Palestine, to a land which, thanks to you, will return to her.*

England knew how to defend its interests better than God His. God had given Palestine and Transjordan in one stroke. Lord Balfour kept Transjordan.

_____

*   Loose translation of Exodus 3:17.

It is true that, in between the two eras, Muhammad had a word to say.

***

The train chugged along. My rabbi dozed. Having slipped slightly, his illustrious hat had uncovered the skullcap he wore beneath it. Every Orthodox Jew wears two headpieces, since a gust of wind or carelessness can separate the first from his head. How indecorous would it be if the name of the Lord (blessed be His name!) was uttered in front of a skullcap-less Jew!

At Chatham, my companion opened his eyes. They were handsome. My man may have hailed from Galicia, but his eyes came from a much more distant place. They were still inhabited by the Orient. Having extracted his Talmud from the wooden case, this Polish subject plunged into Hebrew.

As they ambled down the corridor, the English cast shocked looks at the traveler. You can belong to a tourist nation and not have seen everything. It was his *peyyes* (sidelocks) that stunned them most. The rabbi soon became the center of attention on the train. Those who noticed him pointed him out to their neighbors while the curious, pretending indifference, kept walking past our compartment. An ordinary fellow would have stood up and asked: "What do you want, gentlemen?" But when one flirts with God through difficult printed characters, the mind has no room for stupid creatures.

Calmly, the rabbi mumbled on his text, his lips in motion like a munching rabbit.

***

We arrived in London. The traveler was expected. Two men, dressed in European style, welcomed him without raising their hats. They greeted him with their shoulders, necks, a quivering of nostrils and gymnastics of eyebrows. The trio entered into conversation and, naturally, made gestures. Their robotic hands outlined the content of their thoughts. The gesture is, indeed, the accent of Israel.* A Jew expresses himself as much with his fingers as with his tongue. If he were one-armed, he would be half mute!

They ignored the taxis, left the station and walked.

One of the Europeans carried the case. The rabbi had his Talmud under one arm. The third drew arabesques in the dark with his arms.

Soon they came to a halt. One did not have to be a detective to determine that they were waiting for a bus. After a few smiles from the London crowd, the stately vehicle arrived. We got on. Where were the sons of Abraham taking me? I could see Piccadilly, guessed the entrance to the Strand, then it seemed to me that we were crossing the city. The chatterers spoke faster than the speed of the bus and, when the monster stopped, they continued to chat. The journey came to an end. They got off in front of a big building that, without vouching for it, must have been London Hospital. We were on Whitechapel Road.

It was pretty quiet. I followed them without difficulty. They walked back up the main street, turned into Silver Street, then into Chicksand Street. It was a tiny, somber, clammy street, lit only by the lights of the stores. At number 17, the trio disappeared down a corridor. The house was built of dirty bricks and the ground floor housed a poultry vendor who sold badly plucked ducks and chickens.

---

* Londres uses the term "Israel" to designate the Jewish people, as does the Hebrew language, following the designation of the patriarch Jacob as Israel (Genesis 35:10).

"See you tomorrow," I said to myself as I noted down the address.

I made my way back. The walls of the buildings oozed with damp. Behind the windowpanes, families sat down to meager meals. I was again on Whitechapel Road. As I walked, I noted the shop signs: Goldman, Appelbaum, Lipovich, Blum, Diamond, Rapoport, Saul Levy, Mendel, Elster, Goldberg, Abram, Berliner, Landau, Isaac, Toby, Rosen, Davidovich, Smith, Brown, Lewinstein, Solomon, Jacob, Israel…

And that was just one pavement!

I was deep into my subject.

CHAPTER 2

We Return to Chicksand Street

Twelve o'clock. Two men in the center of London were searching for a kosher restaurant.

"Do you insist on it?" asked one of them.

"We should take advantage, since we are not hungry this morning," I answered.

I was one of the two men. The other was my new companion. I had discovered him that morning, at 77 Great Russell Street, in the Central Office of the Zionist Organization. He, rather than someone else, had been assigned to me, as I wanted someone who spoke Yiddish.

"We could perhaps have lunch at a Lyons Corner House," he said. "The food isn't kosher but at least it's a Jewish firm."

"Today, let us be worthy children of the Lord, your God. Let us eat kosher."

We found a ritual restaurant in the Strand. It was crowded. Some clients were wearing hats. Others had taken their hats off like simple Christians. We sat down. You are certainly acquainted with such establishments. The Hebrew letters, which serve as their emblem, make them distinctive to the eye. They are proof, all over the world, of the attachment of the Jewish people to their laws:

> Do not eat anything that is unclean. Eat of the cow, sheep, kid, stag, wild goat, buffalo, roe deer, oryx, giraffe. You will eat of all animals that have a cloven hoof and chew the cud. You must not eat of those that chew the cud but have no cloven hoof, such as the camel, the hare, and the coney. The swine, too, is unclean unto you, for though its hoof is cloven, it does not chew the cud. Of all the animals that live in the waters, you will eat of those that have fins and scales.*

And many more commandments still.

Thus speaks the Lord in the fifth book of Moses.

And thus millions and millions of Jews still eat.

"And if we tried giraffe meat?" I ventured.

"Examine the physiognomy of this clientele," my companion suggested, "and tell me if there is such a thing as typical Jewish traits, as people claim. There are Jews who resemble the stereotype…"

"You think so?"

"But most…"

"Anyway, it's an honor to the race," I said, "and you see some quite fetching heads."

The meat that we were served looked as though it had been cooked in blotting paper. Not a drop of blood. But let us move on.

"I am not from here," said my companion. "I am a Polish subject born in Russia. But I have a friend who works in the Jewish theater. He could be useful to us. Wait a moment, I am going to find out the address of this theater."

---

*   Loose translation of Deuteronomy 14:3–9.

He questioned our neighbor. The latter, who looked more like a minor English clerk than a free child of Abraham, answered: "Yes, I know that there is a Jewish theater, but I never go there."

He said this with a smile infused with more than a little scorn.

"Another one who is in denial," said the Pole. "Of course, in France, in England… You can see they know nothing about what's going on here."

After having drunk a last glass of ginger beer, a drink that Moses, as a man of taste, had not recommended, we donned our hats and made our way to Whitechapel.

It is in the east of London, in the "East End" – in other words, the end of the East. At a time when Jews, fleeing the persecutions of eastern Europe, settled here, it was the far end of the capital. But the desert never scared them! There is no need for a barrier to mark the entry to Whitechapel or a leaflet warning that you are about to enter a non-English country. You can smell it. It is as noticeable as passing from an icebox to a hothouse. The people who live here are English subjects, or will be, vote like the English, speak English, but, from the very first buildings, nothing smells of England here. It is more human – I was going to say more Latin, forgetting that Latin is not Hebrew! The silhouettes, stamp of the face, darting gazes, general movement, asceticism of some, fat of others, innate curiosity, smell of onions, worry and satisfaction, this is Israel!

They do not hide it. All their famous names, the least known of which is Isaac, are emblazoned above their stores. Fidelity to their origins is one of the attractive features of this tragic people. English? Yes, they are proud of it. From family stories, they know what price their fathers paid for having been born in Russia. So, after being Jewish, they are certainly English. If anyone were to suggest that they leave England, return to the East – that is, immigrate to Palestine – they would answer: "We are English!" Yet, in their imaginations, the ancient Hebrew soil is always soft under their feet. They tread it with delight. What does one see in the windows and inside the stores of Whitechapel Road, Mile End Road, Commercial Road and the beginning of Stepney? Images. One represents the fight between David and Goliath. Further on, vanquished Saul performs hara-kiri on Mount Gilboa. Then there are images of Jerusalem, the entry of General Allenby into Gaza. Nebuchadnezzar carrying off the princes, warriors and judges into captivity. Lord Balfour inaugurating the Hebrew University on Mount Scopus. Is that a portrait of George V presiding over their yearly calendar? No! It is that of the modern-day messiah, the great twentieth-century Jew, the pope of Zionism, Theodor Herzl! This shirtmaker does not possess toggle buttons, but he has on his wall a map of Palestine! And what does one find on their soap, at least on the one I bought? A two-triangle star, the shield of David.

"So, are we going to look for your rabbi?"

"This way," I said.

We found Chicksand Street. While at night, the backstreets of Whitechapel do not warm your heart, during the day they give you a chill in the back. When it is not in the air, the London fog has to be somewhere. So it is here. I found its hideout. It rests on the pavements and on the walls. It condenses itself in order to permeate all the more. As soon as it feels fit again, it rises, not without leaving its trace, then goes off to do its rounds over the capital, after which it will return to scatter itself over the roofs of Whitechapel...

The poultry vendor at number 17 had, again, plucked his birds very badly.

"The name of your man?" the Pole asked me.

"There are no two individuals like him in all of England. His appearance is a name."

The vendor who needed to learn how to pluck had not seen him. The first-floor inhabitants had not heard about him. But at the back of the courtyard, in front of an open window, I perceived the rabbi. Installed in an armchair of red ribbed fabric, head topped by a skull-cap, sidelocks swinging, he was reading with his lips from a big black book.

As I rushed down the stairs, my companion advised me to quash my enthusiasm.

"You shouldn't jump on him. He is a Jew from the East, he is far removed from your way of thinking. Caution is advised."

Since we came on behalf of the Zionist Organization, the welcome given by the hosts was amicable. One of the men who, the evening before, had come to fetch the rabbi at the railway station invited us to sit in the front room. We learned that the strange traveler was, indeed, a rabbi and that his community was situated in Galicia, between Tarnopol and the Romanian border. The inhabitant of 17 Chicksand Street was his grandnephew. The man of God would not refuse to talk to us.

We were introduced to him.

The rabbi closed his Talmud. Without knowing who we were, he held out his hand and said, "Shalom!"

"Shalom!" answered the Pole.

This is the Hebrew greeting, in place of our "hello," and it means "peace be with you."

With the Pole translating for me, I immediately told the rabbi that, having traveled in his company, I had wanted to know his address. This was not out of curiosity, but for a serious reason: I had formulated the idea of describing the state of the Jews in the world to the French; I planned to visit his country, several others, and even Palestine, and I felt that by bringing me in contact with a holy rabbi at the start of my journey, Providence was perhaps telling me that it approved of my enterprise.

"*Todah rabah!*" (Thank you very much!), the rabbi responded.

I inquired as to the goal of his journey to London.

"The plight of my community is great," he answered. "The cold, which is going to last for many long months, will aggravate it. My Jews have nothing to eat and nothing to wear. Children go barefoot on the ice, and the wind pierces through the houses, because they are made of beams and the beams do not join together. I have come to London to collect alms. Jews who enjoy a favorable position must help their brothers who are still oppressed. Is it not we who are closest to Him [God]? Without us, who would still pray to Him?

"If misfortune weighs down on so many children of Israel," he added, "is it not the ransom they pay for the egoistical happiness and impiety of others?"

The grandnephew urged us to consider his granduncle's case. Born in the ghetto, living in the ghetto, the latter probably did not fully understand modern obligations. It may have been sufficient for the Jews of Galicia to please God; Western Jews, alas, also had to please men.

The Pole translated for me what the grandnephew said to his relative: "But we too, Rabbi, as English as we are, we observe the Sabbath. Tomorrow, Friday, with the first star, while all London is still working, you will hear the steel shutters descend on Whitechapel."

"May the Holy Name be blessed! But the truth is the truth," responded the rabbi. "It is not envy that guided my tongue. If there are among you Jews who, unable to resist a century of material comfort, are no more than Israelites,* we want nothing to do with them.

---

*   "Israelite" is a term that was coined in nineteenth-century France to designate Jews in general. It subsequently came to refer to assimilated Jews.

They think they are English, French. They have lost their minds. They have broken the covenant. They have lost everything. For us, they are no longer Jews and, for Westerners, they are still Jewish. But I think of you, Samuel Gosschalk, whose father is still one of ours but who has become English. This entails distancing oneself from one's own people. Danger threatens you. Your children, too, perhaps will be no more than Israelites, since this is what they call you!"

As he translated this heartfelt cry, my Pole made a point of stressing, in his turn, that we were in the presence of a fanatic.

"The problem," he added, "is that there are thousands like him. This is not going to help us find a solution to the Jewish question."

"And Zionism?"

"They reject it. Their rabbis, who decide everything over there, are its worst enemies."

"Ask him, nonetheless, what he thinks of the Balfour Declaration."

The Pole posed the question. The holy man replied: "Mr. Balfour is a lord, not a messiah."

The rabbi returned to his armchair. He picked up his Talmud and, without looking up at us again, oblivious to the fact that Whitechapel was far from the Carpathians, plunged body and soul, sidelocks swaying with celestial fervor, into the commentaries on the divine word.

CHAPTER 3

The Heart of Israel Still Beats

A rabbi from Galicia in London – it is good but not enough. Even though he did not pass unnoticed in Whitechapel, he was submerged by the other Jews. He looked like a picturesque buoy bobbing in an indifferent sea.

No one knows exactly how many they are in the East End. More than a hundred thousand? Anyway, they are a lot! And the anchor they have laid down here seems pretty solid.

"Do you know how my grandfather arrived in London?"

"Where did he come from?" I asked.

"From Lithuania, with two little spoons as his entire fortune. They even say, in the family, that he took them without the knowledge of his family. I don't believe it. He's too honest."

The woman who spoke to me thus was leading me to the house where she was born. We were walking side by side on Commercial Road. Now, she lives on the west side, in a genteel neighborhood. We know that the higher the rent, the more the tenant is respectable! She had been introduced to me the night before, also on the west side, at the home of a well-known lawyer – a Jew and, as he himself said, a British subject. He assured me that the English, knowing his situation, held him more in respect than if he had said that he was English of Jewish faith.

The grandfather was still alive. He was the only one left in the family who still lived in Whitechapel. His children had progressed to better neighborhoods. As for the children of his children, they had moved even higher!

"Here," said my companion as she stopped in front of the window of a jeweler's store. "Here is what has become of the two little spoons from Lithuania."

The grandfather was called Murgraff. As we entered the store, we saw a man seated, head bent over a ledger.

"There's an error of one shilling," his granddaughter cried out. "One shilling – that's a lot!"

Old Murgraff smiled. Forty years in England had done injury to the orthodoxy of his beard, but the race was safe.

After entering into conversation, we soon arrived at the interesting part.

"There is also a Jewish quarter in Paris," he said, "the rue des Roses…?"

"Des Rosiers! Yes. But it's minuscule compared to Whitechapel!"

"Well, I could just as easily be in your rue des Rosiers as I am here in Whitechapel. When, at the age of twenty-five, I arrived here, I wasn't sure I would find a livelihood here. I was ready to go to Paris."

"So now I would be French instead of English," said the prettiest flower of the Murgraff branch.

"That would also be honorable!" the jeweler answered. "And you would live close to the Étoile!"

Why had Murgraff left Lithuania? His story is like that of all the others, all those who live on Commercial Road, and like all those who live on the rue des Rosiers. It is the same today as it was forty years ago. And forty years ago, it was the same as forty years before.

Poland and Romania replaced Russia. But Poland and Romania also bought Russia's stock of anti-Semitism. A Jew, over there, is always a Jew. He may be a man, but he is neither a Romanian nor a Pole. And if he is a man, he is a man who must be prevented from growing. From the entire history of the Jews, eastern Europe retained only the story of Job: "Let the day perish on which I was born, and the night that said, 'A man is conceived.'"* Well spoken! say our Slavic and Latin friends. They believe that Abraham's descendants should remain in the same spot where Job liked to sit. The Jewish problem is complicated but I think it can be summed up in a single question about air: to breathe or not to breathe. No more, no less.

Old Murgraff shared my opinion. The granddaughter, who knew no other environment than that of London, understood less well. She did not have the ability to perceive the entire Jewish world. Of course, she did not deny that she was Jewish, but she seemed to believe that she was a Jew in England like others were Scottish or Welsh. The temple, church, synagogue concerned the soul. And if one does not go to synagogue any more than one's friends go to church or to a temple, the road that leads there is of no consequence. Today, an elegant woman visits God less than she visits her dressmaker. One goes more to the cinema and to tearooms than to services. The same roof unites you around the same pleasure…

This is what the "assimilated lady" tried to explain.

"Child," retorted old Murgraff, "you think like a happy woman who sees no further than her own happiness."

"But you," I said, "forty years in England…?"

"In our case – that of the Jews of England, of France, of Belgium, of the West – there are two stages. I represent one of these, my

---

*   Job 3:3.

granddaughter the other. I am a transplanted tree. My Sarah was born acclimatized. I have the deepest gratitude towards England. These highly intelligent countries viewed us like men, not like some kind of frightening demon. They treated us as equals. It is up to us to show them that they were not mistaken. It is my happiness and not my birth that commands me to love England. It is doubly dear to me: firstly for its lucidity of mind which made it understand that a Jew is not a devil with horns, and secondly for its kindness. I am a faithful British subject. I trembled with pride when my two sons went off to war. The sentiment that overtook me was not the crude satisfaction of paying off a debt to get rid of it, but of doing my duty. Fidelity to the country that welcomed me seemed natural.

"But, dear sir, I am an old Jew. I suckled Hebrew. One of my brothers, over there, still wears a caftan and boots. I feel in me all the sediments of my race. It would be no more worthy of me to deny Israel than to be ungrateful towards England." Raising a hand, old Murgraff pointed to a portrait of Theodor Herzl on his wall.

"You are a Zionist?"

"I am for everything that can lighten the suffering I experienced in my childhood. When one has managed to climb out of a ditch, one must not cut the ropes that can save others."

"Did many from Whitechapel leave for Palestine?"

"Two or three families… But they came back."

There exists, in the intellectual order of things, two species of Zionists: the pure and the less pure. The pure are the apostles who, transported by idealism, burned their bridges and found ones that led them to Palestine. The less pure are the Murgraff type. These are people who are guided more by reason than by enthusiasm. They will help those who wish to cross the Mediterranean but they, themselves, remain on shore. In the same way, candidates for the crossing of the Atlantic sometimes find sponsors…

The pure Zionists left Russia, Poland, Romania. Some also hailed from Belgium, Holland and England.

There were no "pure" Zionists in France.

"So," I said to my Jew, "the heart of Israel no longer beats in Whitechapel?"

"What do you mean?"

"If only two or three families…"

"Ah! The heart of Israel no longer beats in Whitechapel?" Murgraff took his hat, donned it and conveyed an order to his employees.

"I am going to show you something," he said. So we left.

We regained Commercial Road and then I have no idea. Night had already fallen. We walked between two rows of Jewish names. The further we went, the more there were. They reeled in front of my eyes like flip-book images. The race ended at Redmans Road.

It was almost six in the evening. The street was economically lit. Hundreds of children flowed into it from both ends. Here, children were going to school at a time when, everywhere else, they were leaving school. We were surrounded by a swarm of kids. They jumped, ran and disappeared, all of them, into the same abyss. These were little Jewish children who, having finished their English school, were now rushing to their *talmud Torah*.

"Israel!" the jeweler cried out with pride.

After spending their days learning what little English kids learn, the children streamed into this corridor every evening, in order to drum into their heads the fact that they were little Jews.

I was struck by the look of the institution. Bearded rabbis wearing skullcaps and flowing caftans circulated in the middle of this horde of kids in jockey caps. From the very doorstep, it felt as though one were treading on holy ground. To hell with English manners, heads here had to remain covered. Goodbye George V and long live God, King of Israel.

They were six hundred in the building – boys, of course, the daughters of the chosen people having no right to knowledge.

The classes began. In the front of each room, behind the master's desk, stood the ark of the Torah.

The Torah is the law of the Jews. This law consists of the five books of Moses. It recounts what happened from the time of the creation of the world until year 2552 and a half before Jesus Christ. The devotion of Jews to this law has been unfailing. It is their national flag, their patriotic hymn, their unknown soldier. They do not just have respect for the holy Torah, they feel eternal love for it. And among all the beautiful names they have accorded it, one name exudes sublime love: the "crowned bride."

As an object, the Torah is a long scroll held at each end by a wooden roller. The scroll is wrapped around these rollers, enabling it to stand straight in the ark. As for the Torah scribes, the calligraphers of the Law, those wonderful *sofrim*, the moment has not come to present them to you.

The ark of the Torah stood in front of each class, hidden behind a green velvet curtain, decorated with a lion, stag, panther or eagle. This was to remind the children of Israel that they must be strong as a lion, agile as a stag, bold as a panther and swift as an eagle.* Do not interpret these symbolic images as encouraging attributes needed to survive in life – the sole purpose of these attributes is to carry out the will of God.

Standing in front of the ark, the rabbi manipulated a big book. All the children had the same big book on their desks: the Torah. It was not like the scroll in the ark, but the words of Moses printed

---

* Londres references Ethics of Our Fathers 5:23: "Judah, the son of Tema, said, 'Be bold as a panther, swift as an eagle, agile as a stag, and strong as a lion, to do the will of thy Father Who is in Heaven.'"

in Hebrew on stationer's paper. All read aloud, in unison, the rabbi setting the lead and correcting errors. There were more than one hundred in each class, wedged together, squashed like dates in a box. Jews have never had a lot of room. Nations ration them land. Those Whitechapel children were jammed on top of one another like the dead in their distant cemeteries, whose tombstones jostle together so frighteningly.

What do the children learn in these schools? To read the Torah. They begin first to recite the twenty-two Hebrew letters that descended from the crown of the Eternal. The aim is to understand the holy language? No! The aim is to be moved by its intoxicating music. It is the music that imparts wings to the imagination, that transports the spirit to the countries one dreams of. And these children, born in England, of parents born elsewhere, sing the Law, shoulder to shoulder, like the ancient Hebrews. And the map of the Holy Land faces the ark of the Torah…and thus these little souls are already imbued with the Jewish drama…

You were right, old Murgraff, the heart of Israel still beats.

CHAPTER 4

Theodor Herzl

There lies near Vienna, in the Döbling Cemetery, a tomb. The man who inhabits it had an extraordinary destiny. Three thousand two hundred forty-seven years after Moses, he succeeded Moses.

He was more than a king. He had more than a scepter: he had wings. His mission was greater than reigning over a country. At the sound of his voice, borders cracked. His spirit spread across the world. He awoke a people that had slumbered for nineteen centuries.

He was a Jew.

The people were the people of Israel.

The name of the man was Theodor Herzl.

He was born in Budapest in 1860.

It is said that he was Sephardi, in other words, that he descended from Spanish Jews whom the Inquisition had tortured with amorous zeal. He owed the beauty of his face and the majesty of his bearing to this origin. "Like Saul," wrote Zangwill,[*] "he towered over his brethren with his height, his long black beard, sparkling eyes and face of Assyrian kings on ancient friezes. His conversation

---

[*] Israel Zangwill (1864–1926), British Zionist author.

was fascinating and he had a magnetic effect on all those who came into contact with him, from emperors to poor Jews who stopped to kiss the rim of his coat."

He was a journalist in Paris, a correspondent for the Viennese newspaper *Neue Freie Presse*.

His reincarnation took place in 1891. As a law graduate, he had, at first, donned the black robe when he did his traineeship at the court of Salzburg. But the instinct of his race propelled him in another direction. He gave up the robe for a suitcase and went off to discover the world.

On the way, having sent his impressions to several newspapers back home, he caught the attention of *Neue Freie Presse*. It sought him out, found him in Spain and offered him Paris.

The unknown traveler accepted. Veteran French parliamentary journalists need only refresh their memories. They will see our man writing under the staircase of the salle de la Rotonde, in the Chamber of Deputies. Foreign journalists did indeed work under the staircase. It was replaced, in recent years, by an elevator. The new Moses under a staircase! But the president of the chamber is not expected to be a sorcerer!

Herzl was successful. He published a book, *The Bourbon Palace*, which was a hit in central Europe. His plays were staged in Vienna and Berlin. *Neue Freie Presse* appointed him to the post of literary director. Life was beautiful for this beautiful man, when suddenly…

The Dreyfus Affair erupted. In the streets of Paris, he heard cries of "Death to the Jews!"

Until this point, Herzl had lived a dilettante's life. The story goes that, at a young age, he had said to his family's physician: "For us Jews, the only way of forming a respected nation is to leave and go to Palestine."

"And who will take us there?"

To this question, Herzl is said to have replied: "Me!"

Since then, he appeared to have forgotten his mission. Like other members of his race, he had had his bar mitzvah and delivered his first speech in Hebrew in synagogue. The religious manifestations stopped there. And, of course, he believed he was a good Austrian citizen.

The cry of "Death to the Jews!" was like a bolt through his heart. It stopped him in his tracks. "I, too," he said to himself, "am a Jew."

The fact that this cry was heard in France is what particularly shocked him. For over two hundred years, France had recognized Jews as full-fledged men. It stood at the head of the nations in Israel's heart. If, here, the ground suddenly shook under his feet, if the suspicion that rested on one individual was projected onto all, it meant that a Jew, even in this privileged country, was not in his own home.

On that day, Herzl understood his mission.

He turned his life upside down, dropped his successful career and went into a frenzy of activity.

In the first act of his new incarnation, he resumed his profession: he wrote a book.

A book? More a legal text. To the five books of Moses, he added his own. He opened the eyes of his people and told them: "See where you are after nineteen centuries of being on the road." Having confronted them with their situation, he posed the issue of the return to Palestine and, as though on a big blackboard visible to the entire world, in front of fourteen million attentive, dispersed Jews, he wrote down the solution.

The book was called *The Jewish State*.

"I had never written anything before in such a state of exultation," he said. "Heine recounts that he heard the flapping of an eagle's wings over his head when he composed some of his verses. I heard above me something similar to a tremor."

But his book was everything and also nothing. Herzl had laid his base; now he had to erect the monument.

He went on a crusade, none more astonishing in modern times. He rushed to see first Baron Maurice de Hirsch. When you don't have money and you want to create a state, you first have to knock on the doors of money vaults. Baron Hirsch had contributed hundreds of millions to the plight of his people. He had bought for them fifty million marks' worth of land in Argentina. He was a man who was prepared to venture into risky waters.

Herzl meant nothing to the baron. He was just a young man who was going to publish a book. But the person who entered his home was not a beggar, he was the ambassador of future times. When the baron, intrigued by his bearing, entered into a discussion with his guest, Herzl interrupted him, saying, "Let's not waste our time." And, striking the proofs of his book, he declared: "Everything is here!"

"What about the money?" asked the financier.

"I am going to launch a national Jewish fund of ten billion marks," answered the journalist. We are assured that Hirsch answered: "Rothschild will give one hundred pence and the other Jews nothing." The sum of ten billion put an end to the meeting. But the following day, Herzl wrote to Hirsch: "I would have liked to show you my banners and how I intend to deploy them. And if, ironically, you had asked me, 'What is a flag? A rag at the end of a stick?' I would have answered, 'No, sir, a flag is more than that! With a flag, one can lead men to where one wishes, even to the Promised Land.'"*

Baron Hirsch died. *The Jewish State* was published. Herzl went to visit Zadoc Kahn. As chief rabbi of France, Zadoc Kahn had no desire whatsoever to go to Palestine. Herzl, after all, was a foreigner,

---

*   Herzl met with Baron Hirsch in Paris on June 2, 1895.

an Austrian, and he was broaching a formidable subject. It is said that Herzl told him: "All this is of no interest to you? Quite! You are a French Jew? Quite! My project is indeed an internal Jewish matter. So adieu!"

He left for London. He made a big impression and gave several speeches. There, as in Paris, he understood that he was talking in a desert, that poor Jews are the plague of rich Jews and that it is very difficult, even in the name of an ideal, to persuade people, who are comfortably settled, to move.

From these first castings of the net, Herzl brought back only one disciple: Max Nordau.*

The Zionist doctrine that radiated from Herzl had spread across borders. He launched a call for a universal congress. It was the sign that people were awaiting to go on the offensive. The rabbis of London and of Vienna hit out first. The German rabbis, in unison, denounced the false messiah. To stem the current that sought to drown him, Herzl founded a newspaper, *Die Welt*, and answered them with these words: "Synagogue lackeys." The rabbis won. Munich, chosen as the site of the congress, refused to host it. Herzl turned around and chose Basel.

Ah! Those Basel days! What a spectacle! Israel reunited, for the first time in twenty centuries. There were Poles, Hungarians, Germans, French, Russians, English, Dutch, Americans, Egyptians, Mesopotamians, Yemenites, meaning a little dark if not negro. There were clean-shaven faces but also beards and more beards. And sidelocks floating around temples! All these brothers who had never met before, staring at each other in stupefaction! Herzl, in front of

---

*   Max Simon Nordau (born Simon Maximilian Südfeld; 1849–1923), Austrian doctor and author, Paris resident and fellow *Die Neue Freie Presse* correspondent who was to become Herzl's right-hand man.

this living map of the world, trembled. Would his breath be able to mold these souls into one?

He mounted the podium and, before starting, cast his famous gaze at this mass. Then something supernatural took place. The assembly, hesitating for a moment, rose to its feet, fascinated. The dispersed race had just seen the effigy of the race appear. After a quarter an hour of delirium, Ben Ami, giving voice to the unanimous feeling, bellowed the old Hebrew cry: *Yechi hamelech!* (Long live the king!)

***

Herzl traveled to Berlin to see Wilhelm II.* The chancelleries had been impressed by the Basel affair. The emperor was curious about this strange man. He received him. By chance, Wilhelm was preparing a trip to Palestine, with a stop in Constantinople. Herzl traveled to Constantinople. Was not his goal to obtain from the sultan the transfer of Palestine in exchange for cash payment? Who better, then, than Wilhelm to plead the cause with the Grand Turk? For, while it was not common knowledge at the time, Herzl knew that Germany had a stranglehold over Turkey. Wilhelm received Herzl a second time in the Yildiz-Kiosk palace.† This time, Chancellor Bülow‡ participated in the meeting. Herzl already had the allure of a head of state. He just needed a state!

The upshot of these conversations was such that Herzl, flanked by a Zionist delegation, decided not to let Wilhelm get away. Wilhelm

---

*   Kaiser Wilhelm or Wilhelm II (1859–1941) was the last emperor of Germany and king of Prussia, 1888–1918.

†   The elaborate residence of the sultan in Istanbul, Turkey.

‡   Bernhard Heinrich Karl Martin von Bülow (1849–1929), imperial chancellor of Germany 1900–1909.

was going to Jerusalem? Herzl would also go to Jerusalem. He set out. And when, during the emperor's solemn entry into the holy city, Wilhelm noticed Herzl in the crowd from up high on his horse, he bent over the animal and extended his hand to the crownless king. Another meeting, in Jerusalem. The Jews are enthusiastic. Herzl returns to London. Ten thousand Jews jostle to hear him. He announces that the time is near. All of eastern Europe quiver, hands extended toward the messiah.

The days pass. Nothing new on the Jewish horizon. The people murmur.

***

Herzl traveled again to Constantinople to see the sultan. He was going to present him with a charter. The Ottoman court refused him entry to the palace. It wanted to see the gold first, the gold Herzl had talked about. What interested the Turks, in this man, was less the prophet than the alchemist! The prophet won. Abdul Hamid* invited Herzl to the *selamlik*.† After the ceremony, he gave him an audience. The impression that the Jew made on the caliph was immediately evident: "Here is Jesus Christ!" he cried on seeing him enter.

Herzl emerged with hope and the Grand Cordon of the Order of Mejidje.‡ He just needed to find the money. Paris laughed in his face. London promised capital but, beforehand, the English wanted to see the sultan's signature at the bottom of the charter. The sultan, for his part, wanted to set eyes on the money before affixing his signature.

---

*   Abdul Hamid II (1842–1918), sultan of the Ottoman Empire, 1876–1909.

†   The *selamlik* was a portion of the sultan's palace reserved only for men. It can also refer to male guest quarters.

‡   An honorific title bestowed upon him by the sultan.

Herzl failed in his goal, as he tripped over the Jewish bankers' hearts of gold.

He targeted Carnegie,* a man of wealth; Cecil Rhodes,† a businessman. The businessman appeared to bite, but passed away.

Herzl returned to Constantinople. The sultan lodged him in Therapia‡ like a prince, with an aide-de-camp and a carriage. Herzl and the grand vizier entered into negotiations. Herzl wanted the sultan to authorize Jewish colonization in Palestine. The sultan offered other lands in Asia Minor, but reserved Palestine.

For Herzl, this constituted the fall of the last wall of the Temple.

He left for Russia. He saw Plehve.§ He saw Witte.¶ The conversations he had with these men were communicated to the czar. He was told that Russia would allow no movement that would assist the insubordination of Russian Jews but, if it involved reducing their numbers, it would support Herzl.

It is then that Herzl had the Vilna revelation. On his way back, he stopped in Vilna. Vilna is the Jerusalem of snow. Ten thousand Jews surrounded the hotel of the new messiah and cheered him.

The Russian governor called the Cossacks out. The *nagaikas*** entered into action. "What's going on?" asked Herzl. "Why are they beating these people?" It was clear that he had never set foot in these parts before.

---

*   Andrew Carnegie (1835–1919), highly successful American industrialist.

†   Cecil John Rhodes (1853–1902), British businessman and politician in the South African colony.

‡   Tarabya, a neighborhood in Istanbul.

§   Vyacheslav Konstantinovich von Plehve (1846–1904), Russian minister of the interior, 1902–1904.

¶   Count Sergei Yulyevich Witte (1849–1915), chairman of Russia's Committee of Ministers, 1903–1905.

**   Whips used by the Cossacks.

He was escorted to the station, surrounded by Cossacks. Despite the whippings, the Jews rushed to bless him. There were as many floggings as blessings. "This is dreadful," exclaimed Herzl, "dreadful!"

Herzl lost his path. Faced with such events, he compromised on his ideal. With Palestine becoming more remote, other solutions had to be found. He entered into negotiations with the English government for the El Arish region in Sinai. He considered Cyprus. He traveled to Cairo. Everything was crumbling, when…

When the great Chamberlain[*] returned from a trip to Africa. For some time, the Jew had caught the attention of the Englishman. Chamberlain suggested that Herzl should take his people and colonize Uganda! Herzl did not say no.

Then!

Then pandemonium ensued at the Sixth Congress, which took place I don't remember where.[†] Instead of the Promised Land, the negro bushland? The Jews, so André Spire[‡] reported, "tore their clothes, prostrated themselves on the ground, and gnashed their teeth." Jeremiah cursed Herzl.

Pale, Theodor Herzl remained standing. He spoke in a soft voice that calmed the souls. A traitor, him? Oh, my poor children! He declared the vow of love to the homeland and everyone joined him, hands raised, repeating together, like their ancestors when they left for captivity, the oath of the Jews:

If I forget thee, O Jerusalem

Let my right hand forget its cunning

---

[*]   Joseph Chamberlain (1836–1914), British politician and father of the future prime minister Neville Chamberlain.

[†]   The Sixth Zionist Congress took place in Basel in 1903.

[‡]   André Spire (1868–1966), French writer.

Let…[*]

The storm that had shaken Herzl did not abate. To the cry of "Death to the African!" Max Nordau suffered two bullets in Paris.[†] Herzl, who was already sick, did not flee from the storm. He traveled to Rome. He was going to plead the Jewish cause in the Quirinal[‡] and in the Vatican. He saw Tittoni[§] and Merry del Val.[¶] He saw the king. He saw the pope!

He returned to Vienna and convoked the Greater Actions Committee.

"No, my friends," he told the zealots who continued to fire the invective "African" at him, "I am not going to betray you, you can rely on me! Look at me, I am from Zion."

The session ended, Herzl returned home. His breath was fading. He wrote on a piece of paper: "In the middle of life comes death." Then, leaving the paper on his desk, he departed…to render his soul to Edlach.[**]

He was forty-four years old.

Herzl is dead. His dream lives on!

---

[*]   Psalm 137:5, deliberately left trailing off by Londres here.

[†]   This assassination attempt, on December 19, 1903, was inspired by Nordau's spirited defense of the Uganda plan at the Zionist Congress. Londres exaggerates slightly, however, as the bullets missed Nordau.

[‡]   Official residence in Rome of the Italian president.

[§]   Tommaso Tittoni (1855–1931), Italian diplomat.

[¶]   Cardinal Rafael Merry del Val (1865–1930), secretary of state of Pius X, 1903–1914.

[**] Herzl died on July 3, 1904, in the village of Edlach, Austria.

CHAPTER 5

The Journey of the Jews

What a journey is that of the Jews!

They come from time immemorial, from the day when the Lord, designating Abram as the patriarch, changed his name to Abraham. This was, it is believed, around the year 1920 – before Jesus Christ.

On this date too, the Lord promised Abraham to give to his descendants the land where he and his people lived "as strangers" – meaning all the land of Canaan.

Then the circumcision sealed the covenant between God and the Jews.

A little later, famine spread in the land of Canaan. Jacob, son of Isaac, son of Abraham, took his family down to Egypt.

Joseph, son of Jacob, was a great businessman. He became so rich that he bought all the lands of Egypt.

Jacob died. Joseph died. But the great-grandchildren of Abraham multiplied so much that they soon populated the land.

The new pharaoh took note: "See," he said to his people, "the children of Israel have become so numerous they are stronger than us."

He ordered them to be oppressed and the midwives to kill the Jewish males. It was the first pogrom.

It is then that Moses appeared in his basket, among the reeds of the Nile. You know his conversations with God – when he grew up! – and how he led the Hebrews across the Red Sea to the land of Abraham.

But was it the land of Abraham?

I ask this question because it is the burning question of the hour.

Since the San Remo Conference in 1920 (after Jesus Christ), when the Supreme Allied Council gave England the mandate to establish a "Jewish National Home" in Palestine, the Arabs have not stopped creating an uproar.

They deny that Palestine is the cradle of the Jews.

And, as proof, they point to verses 2, 3 and 4 of Genesis, chapter 24:

> And Abraham, being old, said to his eldest servant of his house: "Put, I pray thee, thy hand under my thigh. And I will make thee swear by the Lord, the God of heaven and the God of the earth, that thou shalt not take a wife unto my son of the daughters of the Canaanites, among whom I dwell. But thou shalt go unto my country and to my kindred and take a wife unto my son Isaac."*

Now, this country was Mesopotamia. Abraham, in the eyes of the Arabs, was therefore a usurper!

The Jews took with them from Egypt only the bones of Joseph. After having crossed the Red Sea, they camped in different parts of the plains of Moab, which must have changed its name since then!

---

* All biblical translations are taken from *The Holy Scriptures of the Old Testament: Hebrew and English* (London: British and Foreign Bible Society, 1961).

Moses died. He was succeeded by Joshua. The census of the people established twelve tribes. Nine and a half tribes crossed the Jordan and settled in Palestine. Two and a half tribes remained on the other side of the river, in Transjordan.

Judah succeeded Joshua. And the era of the judges began. Then came the kingdom with Saul, the warrior and the first king. David, Saul's successor, marched toward Jerusalem and captured it from the Jebusites. Consecrated king of all Israel, he planted the flag of the Jews on Zion, meaning he brought the Ark of the Covenant to Jerusalem. Solomon succeeded David and built the Temple. Solomon died. Then the divisions began, followed by a cascade of kings. From Joshua to Herod, meaning in the course of one thousand four hundred forty-five years, war after war subjected the Jews to the Mesopotamians, Moabites, Canaanites, Midianites and Philistines. Then Nebuchadnezzar took them into captivity to Babylon. And the Temple was destroyed. And Cyrus the Persian sent them back to Jerusalem. And the Temple was rebuilt. Then came Jesus Christ. And seventy years later, Titus, sent to Palestine by the League of Nations – pardon, by Vespasian, his father – destroyed the new Temple and sacked Jerusalem.

It is then that the Jews took their walking sticks and set off across the world.

When Titus, back in Rome, exclaimed as was his habit, "I have lost a day,"* it clearly was not of that day that he spoke!

---

* Londres refers to an anecdote written about Titus by the Latin historian Suetonius in 110 CE (*De Vita Caesarum*, "Divus Titus," viii): "[Titus] was most kindly by nature.... On [one] occasion, remembering at dinner that he had done nothing for anybody all that day, he gave utterance to that memorable and praiseworthy remark: 'Friends, I have lost a day.'" J. C. Rolfe, ed., *Suetonius*, 2 vols., The Loeb Classical Library (London: William Heinemann, and New York: The MacMillan Co., 1914), II:321–39.

Where did they go?

There were some who were afraid of water, others who were not.

The first, who were not numerous, dispersed in the direction of Babylon or Arabia. A small group never left the Promised Land. Their descendants, who adopted Arab customs, can still be seen today, in a village in the Upper Galilee called Peki'in!*

The masses sailed away in galleys.

One can assume that a few, among these masses, landed in various parts of the Mediterranean coast. The largest convoy, however, reached Western shores, known today as the shores of Spain and of France. I would like to be able to tell you what they did there but I don't know.

They probably journeyed with no itinerary, spurred by despair and stopping only to straighten their beards when the wind blew them backwards. I can see them divided into numerous columns, following streams and rivers, preceded by a leader who, alone, carries something: a parchment scroll, the Law!

Were they happy during the first eight centuries of our era? I hope so. In contrast, I can feel the distress that must have engulfed them when they learned that the papacy had instructed Charlemagne to transform the West into an empire where Christianity would reign supreme.

The leaders unraveled their scrolls. The Jews grouped around the Law. They read and reread it. No mistake, their law opposed the orders of Charlemagne. Now they were going to enter into conflict with the emperor of the lands on which they treaded!

---

* In addition to Peki'in, sites of continuous Jewish settlement since the destruction of the Temple by the Romans in 70 AD existed in Jerusalem, Hebron and Tzfat.

And so the new passion of the Jews began. The cross that they had hewed for Jesus began to hound them.[*] Charlemagne died. Centuries passed. Europe was carved up. Irrespective of who reigned in the countries where they settled, they were crushed by the cross and its ever-growing shadow.

They were surrounded by hostile nations. Their arrival was greeted by murmurings of the masses. The Torah was in danger. They could no longer camp among the Gentiles with ease of mind. They stopped where they were in order to lie low. If fear opens one's eyes, it also narrows one's horizons, so they crammed together in the same neighborhood. This was the birth of the ghetto, the homeland of homelands. It was the era of the Middle Ages.

From being gypsies, if one can call them that, they became curious creatures. On Sundays, the Christians would roam around the ghettos, like people roam today around animal cages in zoos. Stupidity never takes long to emerge. The Jews took on the appearance of terrestrial demons. Imagination soon gave them tails on their backs, horns on their heads and flames on their lips. No one doubted that they were afflicted with the foulest diseases. From the moment they opened their mouths, the air was poisoned. Their bones pierced through their flesh. Worms ate them alive. Fathers married daughters. On certain dates, they devoured the children of Christians. And if the plague erupted, they were to blame!

So the authorities imprisoned them in the neighborhoods where they had voluntarily cloistered themselves. And, to mark them out, they were obliged to wear a yellow badge on their sleeves.

---

[*]   Although the New Testament is sometimes read as indicating Jewish culpability in Jesus' crucifixion, as of the Second Vatican Council (1962–1965), the Roman Catholic Church has repudiated that belief. The first-century historian Josephus refers to the crucifixion of Jesus by the Romans in *Antiquities* 18:3.

They were mainly in Spain and Germany.

Inquisition Spain wanted to force them to give up the Torah. Many became Christian, not out of love of Christ, but out of fear of Torquemada. They were called Marranos. Ultimately, Spain chased them away. Some reached the Netherlands, others took to sea. The latter could be seen in Salonika, in the era of Sarrail.*

At about the same time, the Jews of Germany took up their walking sticks again. The country had been devastated by cholera, and they were blamed for the disaster. So they traveled to Poland, dragging their ambulatory ghettos along the high roads.

One hundred years, two hundred years went by. Then a star from the Orient shone, one night in the seventeenth century, over the darkest ghettos. Was it, finally, the long-awaited star of the Messiah? Was Israel about to fold its tents and return to the land of Canaan? Everything was possible. This star was none other than a Jew from Smyrna called Shabbetai Zvi. His mad history as a false prophet set off such a storm among the entire Jewish people that even the tough Grand Turk took note. Summoned to Constantinople, Shabbetai Zvi preferred not to be hung. The precursor of Theodor Herzl converted to Islam! The winds of hope fell. And the tents of the ghettos, which had prematurely flapped with joy, subsided, once again, on foreign soil.

It should be noted that not all the Jews lived among the flocks that grazed the West. In Spain as in Germany, in Poland as in Ukraine, intelligence, which always triumphs, carried many of them to the highest places. By prohibiting them all participation in the life of states and relegating them to the impious gold trade, the Church had unwittingly prepared masters of state. Some became

---

*   General Maurice Sarrail commanded the French army of the Orient in Salonika during WWI.

chancellors of Spain, others secret ministers of German princes. Nor did the Polish lords underestimate their talents. But by serving the great, one antagonizes the people. The contempt of the populace soon gave way to hatred. So much so that the most horrible thing happened: Chmielnicki, hetman* of the Ukrainian Cossacks, passed through all the ghettos and massacred three hundred thousand Jews.

So, for consolation, Israel plunged itself into the *Zohar*, meaning that the Baal Shem Tov had appeared.

The Baal Shem Tov lived two centuries ago. He worked as a woodcutter in the Carpathians. And it is upon this companion of wolves that the Lord deigned to descend.

"Abandon your ax," He told him. "Take a wagon, cross the Carpathians, go to Poland and tell My Jews that they no longer know how to talk to Me. Their souls are sad like their garments. For fear of meeting My gaze, their eyes are fixed on the ends of their boots. They cry, they moan. Bent under I know not what burden, they will soon walk on all fours. This people, who should be joyous at being My chosen ones, are steeped in affliction. The light fades from the faces of My Jews and their beards droop on their chins. Tell them that I command them to raise their heads. Instead of moaning, they will sing; instead of trembling, they will dance; instead of fasting, they will make merry."

The Baal Shem Tov laid down his ax. He got on a wagon and set out across Poland. Beating on the doors of synagogues, he cried, "Hey! What are you doing with your foreheads on the ground?

"I have brought you the word of the Eternal. Get up and dance, eat, drink, smoke, sing! Let your mind rest; it has shriveled for having quibbled too long. Your heart is fresh; listen to its desires.

---

*   *Hetman* was Londres's choice of words here, even though he uses *ataman* elsewhere. Both words signify a Cossack leader.

"Close the Talmud! What is it? At the most, an old book of sorcery written by obsolete academicians. Here is the 'in book': the *Zohar*, the book of splendor! Open it and read!'"[*]

Israel, almost in its entirety, listened to the Baal Shem Tov.[†] It read the magnificent *Zohar*. Then it began to pray by dancing, eating, drinking, smoking, singing. It was the birth of Hassidism. And Hassidism gave birth to miracles. And the Baal Shem Tov, known as the Baal Shem, the woodcutter from the Marmarosh Mountains, became the first miracle-making rabbi. And...

Then came the French Revolution. The French taught the world that the Jew was a man, not a demon with horns. But Europe is made of barriers, and the news could not travel across them all. With difficulty, it reached Vienna. Thus, the Jews found themselves split in two. Those of the West, ours, you know. Let us go and see the others!

---

[*] Londres misrepresents the position of the Baal Shem Tov, who emphasized a personal relationship with God regardless of one's scholarly ability but did not discourage Talmud study or encourage popular reading of the *Zohar* (an arcane work written in Aramaic, as is the Talmud).

[†] There was actually a robust opposition to the Hassidic movement, largely due to the discomfort with any charismatic leader after the disaster of the false messiah Shabbetai Zvi. Hassidism did eventually flourish, mainly in eastern Europe.

CHAPTER 6

Here They Are!

When it is thirty-six degrees below zero, you have to shave your moustache – otherwise it becomes too heavy and weighs you down. You no longer have hair under your nose, but icicles. The more you blow to make them melt, the bigger they get. Animal vapor cannot win against the cold of Bohemia.

So, like a snowman, I traveled around Prague. One can shave, but one hesitates to cut off one's nose, ears or the ten toes of one's feet. Mr. Osusky, the Czech minister, who had sent me to the far end of his country under the pretext that, if I wanted to see Jews, that is where I would find them, had clearly told me: "Cover yourself!" Dear Minister, I was wearing three pairs of woolly socks one over the other, gaiters and thick boots. As for ears, I saw your compatriots hiding theirs under a sort of headphone-earmuff.

I was brought up in France, meaning with a revulsion for phones. And even if a headphone ends in two cute velvet muffs, I will reject it. I could, I concede, have bought such a contraption, but what about my nose? I had a scissor holder in my luggage, but then I risked being arrested in the street and placed in a madhouse. That would have been a pity: Prague under snow is such a beautiful lady!

I had come to Prague to visit the Jewish cemetery and synagogue. They represent the oldest signs of Jewish life in Europe. At the entrance to the ghetto countries, they are the two great milestones to the messianic road of the West.

It is not a cemetery but a mass of gravestones, a jostling of stones and tombs. One can see the Jews – I mean one can imagine them – trampling over each other, suffocating in order to find not a place in the sun, but a hole in the ground. Whatever their numbers, when alive, they all had to find room in the ghetto and, when dead, they all had to lie in the cemetery. Neither one nor the other was ever enlarged. It was already an achievement to have been granted a parcel of Christian soil.

Armed with their Hebrew letters, the steles engage in battle, seizing each other around the waist to better uproot their opponents. Some, weary from the struggle, support each other; many have fallen, defeated, and the pile they form testifies to the fierceness of the battle. Others, in order to definitively ensure their position, dive straight into the ground. The most determined push in every direction, tilting to the right, to the left, straddling ferociously over one another. And we are only talking about the top level, about those who gained the upper hand because seven to eight layers of dead inhabit the enclosure. This is not a place of rest but a macabre tumult.

Pigeons, lions, bears, bouquets, one flower, grapes, small pots, crossed hands, roosters, wolves, little cows – all these are sculpted on the stones, as symbols of a tribe or a name. Before Maria Theresa of Austria, the Jews did not have official names. When the empress decided to register them, they had to be "baptized" (meaning, given family names). But Germany, Bohemia and Hungary did not allow the Jews to adopt the sacred names that appear on their calendars. Was it not a dangerous condescension already for a Jew to have a name? To attenuate the impact, they were only allowed to take names of objects or animals. The poor only had the right to the name of a common beast. Those who possessed a few Kreuzer were allowed to choose as their patron a noble, even a fierce animal. Those who possessed gold could choose the name of a flower. In this way, the rich became Blum while the proletariat was no more than a Schwein, meaning "swine."

The happiest of all the dead were those from the tribe of Aaron. Their nobility prohibiting them from dwelling in these unsavory places, they were buried at the edge of this battlefield.

A hundred meters from the cemetery, one can see the synagogue. It is small. But that is not what makes it distinctive. So what is? It seems to be wearing a mask. Indeed, it is Gothic. What had been constructed for these unfortunate people was a synagogue that resembles a church! The architect, a Christian, had shaped the ribs of the vaulted ceiling in the form of a cross! This temple contradicted its god. Subsequently, the Jews added a fifth branch with motifs to blur the sacrilegious sign.

You do not need a powerful imagination to feel the distress of this accursed people hovering over these miserable stones. The mind can easily envisage them as they once were, and as they are still elsewhere, gathered around this house of prayer. Chased, beaten, mocked, unable to leave their concentration camp, accused of witchcraft, sorcery, illnesses, their garments marked with a yellow badge, they walked stooped, pale and thin, beards flowing, down the little alleys of yore, with big strides, heads bent, toward this old synagogue. It was their sole homeland. Only here did they find comfort for their souls. Beneath its vaults and amid the exalted wait for the Messiah, they forgot the evil kings of the day. For them, and just for a few hours, it was like our Truce of God of the year 1000 which prohibited violence from Wednesday to Monday.* When they emerged from the synagogue, they raised large questioning eyes and looked at the time on the Jewish clock, whose hands turn counter-clockwise. How was it that they did not walk backwards?

There was also the Christ on Charles IV Bridge. It is the third witness of Prague's ancient Jewish life. It happened in 1692. A Jew crossing the Vltava spat at Jesus on the cross. The villain was condemned to death and the ghetto forced to atone for the insult. The Jews gilded the Christ and, since that day – supreme reparation – the cross bears the Hebrew inscription: "Holy, three times holy, the name of Jesus Christ."

***

I am going to take the train. I am leaving the civilized world to descend into ghetto country. The hotel porter gave me a small bottle which I have with me, in my pocket. It is not meant for drinking; it is not for getting drunk on but to rub on: it is kerosene. As soon as the tip of my nose becomes white, this means that massage time has arrived. But I do not possess a mirror: so how will I be able to observe the color of my appendage? Perhaps kind-hearted travelers will do me the favor?

I travel first to Mukachevo. When Europe is not under polar ice, Mukachevo is twenty-four hours from Prague. Otherwise it is hard to say. Before the war, this area was Hungarian; today it is the far end of Czechoslovakia. But it is called Subcarpathian Russia, when, in fact, it is Ruthenia…

---

* The Truce of God was a Catholic movement that attempted to limit the violence of regional feuding by placing limits on the number of days during which fighting was possible.

Nothing to note for eighteen hours. My nose is still there. Here is Batu.* Adieu to the beautiful Bucharest railway track! Now, a local train will carry me and fling me into the Carpathians.

And here they are! Here are the Jews! At first glance, they looked to me like extraordinary figures who had descended this morning from the most distant planet, but these were indeed Jews. They formed black silhouettes against the snow, and their beards and caftans made them look like cypress trees. With beards and caftans flapping in the wind, these cypress trees trembled. Well, I confessed to myself, amazed, I had never imagined such a sight. Ah! What ignorance – you who thought you knew every species of man that treads the earth! And this species lives in Europe, forty-five hours from Paris?

Worried (about what?), they wandered across the platform, rummaging everything with their eyes, prowling, prying and questioning. They reminded me of town dwellers in times of war, ducking to avoid enemy planes buzzing over their heads. These Jews seemed to be searching for the nearest shelter and yet they remained outside. They carried bundles over their shoulders or little boxes in their hands. You expected them to offer you their merchandise, like Arabs with their carpets. And when a pair engaged in conversation, their puppet-like hands expressed their words so well that, from afar, one had the impression of taking part in their gesticulating chatter.

I took out my camera and got ready to shoot. Did you ever throw a stone at a group of sparrows? My Jews flew away. Would I ever find any so beautiful? I pursued them with my instrument. Some ran, others hid their faces with their hands, the most brazen showed me their fists. "It doesn't devour men," I shouted. "It's painless!" Since, in these countries, people speak eleven languages, of which the best

---

*   Bátyu, formerly in the kingdom of Hungary, then Czechoslovakia during the interwar period. Today it is called Batiovo or Bat'ovo and is part of Ukraine.

known are Ruthenian, Czech, Hungarian and Yiddish, my French got me nowhere.

They clearly saw that I was not a child of the Lord. I had, indeed, forgotten the commandment of Sinai: "You shall not make for thyself any image or any likeness of any thing that is in heaven above or in earth below…"* I stuffed my camera in my pocket. They returned alongside the train. But their eyes were full of suspicion.

For half an hour I was the object of interminable whisperings. They examined me furtively, passing in front and behind me and walking past again. Their curiosity about me was intense and gushed from their eyes. They were dumbfounded. What sort of a biped could I possibly be? What new misfortune was about to befall them? In far-flung Japanese villages, I had not been stared at with eyes as distrustful as these.

Finally, they boarded a local train. I boarded it, too. They were nineteen, returning to Mukachevo. They crammed into two compartments. I entered a third, separated by a strip of ornamental metal.

The train departed.

There was nothing left in this country except for our train and the snow. The white steppes stretched endlessly up to the mountains, and the white mountains stretched endlessly up to the sky. Suddenly, I heard a kind of chant filling the adjoining compartment – a dark, haunting chant. I stuck my forehead against the ornamental metal. One of the meditating cypresses was standing in a corner. Eyes closed, sidelocks swaying wildly, his face visited by ecstasy, his body rocking with the regularity of a pendulum, he intoned. The others, who were also standing, backs arched, heads tilted, eyelids lowered, shaking from top to toe, moved their lips.

---

*   Exodus 20:4.

The leader of the group became more and more animated. Pious excitement filled the carriage. The tone of confidentiality was followed by the imperious voice of the believer. Now he no longer advised, he commanded. The more he felt his group moving closer to God, the more he pushed them.

The assembly fell into a trance. It seemed to me I was hearing the calls and responses of wild litanies. Beneath still-closed eyelids, burning inspiration pierced through their gaze. Had they continued to shake, the Carpathian Mountains would have crumbled in their midst – not because of the impact, but because of the glory of the God of Abraham, Isaac and Jacob.

The sun was about to set.

They were reciting the Minchah* prayer.

---

*   Afternoon prayer.

CHAPTER 7

And This Is Only Mukachevo!

But where do they come from?

Suddenly, there they are in their Subcarpathian Russia?

Ah! My eyes, do you complain? Do you not see something new?

Abraham, are these your children?

And this is just Mukachevo! What do the ravines and summits of the Carpathians hide?

Who showed them the route to this country? What angel of the night led them here? Misfortune or fear? Both.

They fled from Moravia, from Little Poland, from Russia. Some in former times, some in recent times, chased by the law, hunger and massacres. When you don't have a homeland and a country drives you away, where do you go? Forward. The most recent, who came from Bessarabia, wanted to go to America. This is their America!

In Moravia, only one in each family was accorded the right to marry. It was a smart idea if you wanted to amputate the race. Famine chased them from the banks of the Dniester. And since 1882, fifteen to sixteen hundred pogroms in Russia put the survivors on the road.

They come from there.

The land here was terribly poor, practically virgin. When they pricked up their ears, all they could hear was the howling of wolves and the rustling of the wind among the fir trees. So they came to a stop, thinking that here they would not bother anyone.

They were not Israelites, but Jews. I emphasize this because it needs to be understood. At some point or another, assimilated Jews – whether French, English, German, Dutch or Hungarian – renounced the purely Jewish life. They belong much more to the West than to the Orient. The countries that they adopted and loyally served profited from their genius. And now they are French Jews, just as one is a French Protestant or Catholic. To our genius, they added theirs. That is all one can say.

Those from Moravia, Poland and Russia, our Carpathian Jews, are not Israelites, but Hebrews. They are Hebrew more than Déroulède* was French. And it is this Hebrew life that they came to these mountains to hide – the same life, with adjustments that accentuate even further their distinctive character, that their ancestors led when they came out of Egypt, fifteen hundred years before Jesus Christ.

In what place did they shield themselves from the European contagion? In the ghetto.

It was their refuge. There, they forgot the insults; there the stings of the whiplashes were able to heal. There they no longer met with affronts, mockery, spits. The monarchs of the day had barricaded them together. And since the sixteenth century, they did not leave the ghetto. In this way, they reconstructed, in thousands of fragments, the homeland they had lost at a time when our era was barely one hundred years old.

---

*   Paul Déroulède (1846–1914) was a French author and politician who was one of the founders of the French nationalist organization La Ligue des Patriotes.

On what and how did they survive in these ghettos? They survived on dreams. You just have to look at them if you don't believe me. They are not thin – they are hollow, with pale cheeks and sunken stomachs. If you were to tap them with your fingers, they would resonate like a violin case. Their dreams are filled with nothing but corn, wild fruits, dried vegetables and slaughterhouse scraps from lungs to guts.

Their professions? They had none. You know that the Middle Ages, led by the Church, did not allow them to follow any profession except that which Christians could not practice without sullying themselves: trading in gold. On the other hand, the Talmud forbade them from digging foreign soil.* So what was left for them? To work as retailers or intermediaries and, not owning their own businesses, run the businesses of others, from the smallest to the biggest. For example: I have arrived in Mukachevo. Fascinated by the revelation of this new world, I remain standing on the platform. Ruthenian peasants are unloading carts of wood. A dozen Jews are on the lookout, their beards frothing with excitement. The Ruthenian peasant is not particularly smart. He chopped his wood and brought it; what more can one ask of him? The Jew will sell it for him. The carts come to a stop. Bargaining begins between the peasant, dressed entirely in white wool, and the Jew in his raven's plumage. Agreement is reached quickly. The Ruthenian wants so much. My Jews run off with great strides. They enter stores, climb floors, kicking the hems of their caftans with their shins. One of them, not wanting to neglect anything, makes his way back...and offers me the deal!

---

* The Talmud does not contain such a restriction. The laws of the country banned Jews from owning land.

In 1870, the Hungarian government, in its desire to Magyarize the Carpathians, ordered the Jews to renounce their identity as a people, abandon Yiddish, reform their religion, don our elegant jackets and our handsome trousers and cut off their sidelocks. The intellectuals agreed; the masses refused. The former are now living in Budapest as doctors, lawyers, bankers, public officials and officers. They have become fiercely nationalistic, Hungarian to the extreme. They rejected the Hebrew people, then betrayed it. As Jews of the first rank, they helped Hungarians subjugate the second rank.

But here, deep in the Subcarpathian Mountains, the Jews remain ever faithful to Moses. Rejected by the Hungary that they had rejected, their bodies dwell here but their souls dwell elsewhere. Where? With the *Wunderrabbi.** The Wunderrabbi is a sorcerer rabbi, a miracle maker.

The Wunderrabbis made the Jews as we see them. It is they who prevent them from assimilating and from emigrating.

They tell them: "If you go to impure countries, you will no longer be able to observe the holy Sabbath. Your *peyyes* [sidelocks] will be cut off, you will not see the prophecies fulfilled and God will cast an angry eye upon you. If you send your children to modern schools, your hair will fall out, your sons will become blind and your daughters will commit sins. If you study anything other than the divine word [they do not study geography or arithmetic, nothing; only how to read the Torah and the Talmud], the last wall of the Temple precinct will fall in Jerusalem. The Torah will dry up in its ark and the Messiah will delay his coming."

Are they still waiting for the Messiah? Yes! This is why everything else means nothing to them. Laugh in their faces, pack them in special wagons, prohibit them from owning land, but do not touch

---

*   German, meaning "wonder rabbi."

their Sabbath, or their Torah, or their curls, for the Lord said: "You shall keep my Sabbaths and reverence My sanctuary. Ye shall not round the corners of your heads, neither shalt thou mar the corners of thy beard."*

Miracles are not an issue of kilometers. The two sorcerer rabbis who operate in Subcarpathian Russia live in Romania – one in Vizhnitz and the other in Sighet. The power struggle that they wage here is fierce. Each considers the other a charlatan. They seek to destroy each other with accusations of false prophecy.

One morning, in the Carpathians, the rabbi of Sighet is said to have predicted that the snow would no longer cover the ground on such and such a day at such and such a time, or that the *dibbuk* (a soul tormented by death) would be reincarnated in such and such a person. The followers of the rabbi of Vizhnitz had spread this rumor. And since none of this happened, the holiness of the rabbi of Sighet was compromised. The tactics went beyond spirituality. The devotees of Sighet poured kerosene in the wells of the believers of Vizhnitz. Those of Vizhnitz wrecked the vegetable plots of those of Sighet. Miraculous sand from Sighet penetrated into the sacks of corn of Vizhnitz…

And there were many other miracles!

The laws of the Torah forbid believers from having their affairs resolved by nonbelievers. In these communities, the rabbi is the judge as much as the priest. I am referring to community rabbis. The Wunderrabbis are too preoccupied with the prophet Elijah to interest themselves in petty affairs! The Talmud serves as the code of law, and the community rabbi bases his decisions on it. All cases of civil law pass through his hands. If the case concerns a renegade, he is denounced publicly as a sinner. On the Sabbath, he is requested

---

*   Leviticus 19:30, 27.

to appear in synagogue, where he is excommunicated. Does he balk? The rabbi ascends the pulpit and, in front of a medieval crowd shaking with fear and compassion, the priest of the Talmud, from atop his pulpit, begins to thunder and pronounces, in a last-judgment voice, the formula of excommunication. Around candles blackened in a sign of mourning, the believers recite prayers for the dead. And in the dark, fiery temple, the Jews, possessed by Jeremiah, utter piercing lamentations.

The fate of the renegade is settled. No one will speak to him anymore.

The rabbi is also a doctor, vet, lawyer-consultant, midwife and matchmaker. He has powers over commerce and sterile women. He is the great sorcerer of Israel.

***

It is snowing on Mukachevo. Night approaches. The cold pushed me into my room. But as soon as I entered it, I went out again: the Jews were just so beautiful! And they had become more extraordinary than ever. Now, they were promenading on their heads a hat to top all hats – a big black velvet cake trimmed with rabbit tails. The headgear overshadowed the rest of the costume. It dominated everything. The velvet caftan, however, was not bad either! It was their Sabbath dress.

They no longer walked with big strides. From the appearance of the first star on Friday night till the first star on Saturday night,[*] every activity cedes place to God. Israel is prohibited from traveling, entering a vehicle, carrying loads, smoking and even running. Were the white-dressed Ruthenian peasants to bring a convoy of carts of

---

[*]   The Jewish Sabbath begins at sunset on Friday night and ends when three stars can be seen in the sky on Saturday night.

wood, the black-dressed men would just gaze at the loads from up high, from the shadow of their crowns of thirteen rabbit tails, their stomachs most probably empty, but their souls filled with the Lord.

Where does this costume come from? Not from Jerusalem, surely. Rabbits are not in fashion in hot countries. It is said that this outfit resembles the costume of thirteenth-century German traders. In any case, for a costume, it is some costume.

Night has fallen. These ghosts haunt this extraordinary little town. Bizarre shadows hugging alleyways, they dodge in and out like hares scurrying to their dens. I trail two of these human beings. They disappear under a vault and enter a sort of farmhouse that gives onto a country path. I approach and look through a frosted window pane. What an amazing spectacle! Around a five-branched menorah, thirty Sabbath hats, that is three hundred ninety rabbit tails, sway furiously to the sound of chanting from thirty beards. It is a house of prayer. As he rushes in, a latecomer discovers me peering. He takes three steps backwards. He is afraid of entering. Who is this stranger? Is misfortune about to befall Mukachevo? He leaps into the holy farmhouse. The door slams shut. I step back. The Jews come to the door and stare at me, anguish in their eyes. Pray in peace, sons of Abraham, the stranger is not malicious!

Where am I? In what unearthly country? And those over there with their black sleeves falling over the tips of their fingers – what are they doing, those stuffed ghosts, standing on street corners like scarecrows? Are they perhaps there to scare the snow?

CHAPTER 8

The Feral Jews

So, where am I? Territorially, in Czechoslovakia. There are treaties to confirm this. Here, Czechoslovakia juts against Hungarian, Romanian and Polish borders. It is the region of the great forests of the southern Carpathian slopes. In short, the Marmarosh Mountains.

Spiritually, however, the area is much more distant. It is not in the twentieth century. It has barely passed the age of Genesis. We are in the second era of the world, in the period of the Exodus. President Masaryk, who was one of the first to perceive a drop of prophetic oil* in Zionism, knows very well that when he comes to Mukachevo, to Uzhgorod, to Khust, the governor who receives him is not alone on the station platform. An immense, immeasurable figure accompanies the dignitary, enveloping him with his gigantic shadow. His height dominates the Carpathians, his beard sweeps the ground and his sunken eyes express the long torment of a people: it is Moses!

---

* Ancient prophets read the future from the designs created when oil was mixed with water.

I am now traveling with two Jews with no beards and no sidelocks. One was born in Vilna (Poland),* the other in Transylvania. But they are Czech subjects. This is what they wanted. Czechoslovakia is the only country that grants Jews the right to be Jews, just as Slovenians are Slovenians, and Czechs, Czechs. They take part in national life without being forced to assimilate. If Czech skies were to rain down manna, the Marmarosh Mountains would be the false Promised Land, awaiting the real one. But the sky of this region is less generous than its governors.

One of my companions is called Ben, the other Solomon. They are not Orthodox Jews, meaning that, while respecting the sacred texts, they do not put them into practice; they have more trust in the Balfour Declaration than in the coming of the Messiah; and, furthermore, they do not consider the rabbi as the indisputable incarnation of the divine word. From the point of view of Rome, they would be considered free thinkers; from the point of view of Jerusalem, they are Zionists. On no account Israelites. They see only race, not religion, in a Jew.

Ben and Solomon took charge of me at Mukachevo. They are both frighteningly intelligent. In addition, they speak Russian, Czech, Polish, Romanian, Hungarian, English, Italian, Spanish, German, French, Yiddish and Hebrew. I made their acquaintance in my Mukachevo inn. Hat on my head, my overcoat collar pulled up to my ears, three woolly socks tucked nicely into each of my boots, I was eating one evening, on a once-white tablecloth, the bitter bread of solitude. In a corner, a few Russians were not even drinking! They were playing dominoes, silently, and the cracking of their bones evoked a dance of skeletons. A lady, sitting alone at a table, a woolen shawl over her shoulders, gazed obstinately at the

---

*   Vilna, the capital of Lithuania, was annexed by Poland in 1922.

ceiling as though the Holy Spirit were about to descend. Two men were sipping piping hot tea.

This little family was sitting quietly when a tall Ruthenian, elongated further by his tall grey astrakhan hat, entered, carrying on his back what looked like the coffin of a child. He deposited the box, opened it and took out a parrot. He placed the bird on his forearm, held out a begging bowl in one hand and, with the other, proceeded to turn the crank of his musical coffin. He was one of those troubadours of the snow so prized in Slavic countries, a *charmantka* player! Having ground out his song, he brought me the parrot. The creature dug its beak into the begging bowl, seized a piece of paper and let it drop mournfully on my plate. It told my fortune in Ruthenian. The sugar-bread man rolled out another song. This done, he brought me the bird again. Five minutes later, he whisked the feathered creature under my nose. At this point, I said, "B—— off with your parrot!"

Straightaway, I saw the ears of the tea drinkers tilt in my direction. Their eyes, at the sound of French, were full of astonishment. They exchanged a few words. Then one of them, the redheaded one, got up and, preceded by a restrained smile, asked me if I came from Paris.

"Yes, I do," I answered.

He made a sign to the other, a dark-headed man. They apologized for the curiosity that propelled them, but they had only ever encountered one other Frenchman in Mukachevo, Mr. André Spire!

"There are parrots here," I said, "so why wouldn't there be Frenchmen?"

They answered that parrots were not so rare here. Strapping fellows who try to convince you that parrots live in the Carpathians are not to be ignored. I invited them to sit with me.

"I have come to see Jews," I told them.

"My name is Ben," said the redheaded one, "and my friend is called Solomon."

"So, shalom!"

They answered, "Shalom!"

I wanted to know why they did not have sidelocks. They wanted to know whether French Jews had them.

I inquired as to their professions. Ben was an electoral official and Solomon an insurance agent. Did he insure the purity of beards and the rabbit tails of hats? They leaned on the table and told me that what I had seen in Mukachevo was nothing. I should go up on the mountain, where the feral Jews had their nests. My eyes would be shocked. It was the country of hunger.

The next day, a car made its way up the Marmarosh Mountains. Ben and Solomon were at my side. From Mukachevo we traveled to Batu, from Batu to Khust. Now we were driving toward...toward...

"Where are we going, Ben?"

First to Bushtyna.

The area was mummified by the winter. The snow suffocated everything. The icy road cracked under the iron chains around our wheels. First we saw a group of Ruthenians, dressed in tight trousers and boleros, both in white wool. They were singing as they walked. Their pointed sheepskin hats made them look like candles topped by an extinguisher. A little further on, a bent, black back tramped in the snow: a Jew. Black and white, like a game of draughts, so as not to confuse the pieces!

Bushtyna, our first nest. We had left the car behind and were walking toward an ill-assorted group of huts. It was a camp rather than a village. One-story huts with sloping roofs. The Jews emerged. Hands tucked in their sleeves, they all looked as though they were holding stovepipes against their chests. Should we stop? They surrounded us as though we were a brazier, then suddenly disappeared, fearing being burned, no doubt.

It was the craziest assortment of heads that shoulders have ever born! Neptunes, patriarchs, Rembrandts, goats, young and old vultures, bearded horses and Raphaels! Some of the heads seemed to emerge from the clouds, others from a devil's box! From the earthly paradise to the zoological garden!

"The rabbi's house?" asked Solomon.

Preceding us, but at a distance, they indicated that we should follow them…

One side of the roof of the rabbi's house had disappeared with the wind. We entered a stable: two sheep, two small children, five bigger ones already sporting sidelocks, a skeletal woman, a cageless black bird shivering on the back of a chair.

The rabbi was absent; he had gone to Romania…to beg! The misery of these nests is such that, in order to beg, the famished must travel a hundred kilometers. On home turf, one does not beg – everyone would be beggars then. No one has a farthing more than his neighbor, who has nothing. It is egalitarian misery. They live off it like off an ancestral heritage, their souls without remorse, their spirits tranquil. Their inheritance cannot be contested. The will of Israel is legal!

The woman, hanging onto Ben's coat, moaned in Yiddish.

"What is she saying?"

"She says that she suffers from hunger," Ben answers me.

She showed us some meager fruits and peeled one: one-quarter flesh, three-quarters pit. No more corn in the region. If the rabbi did not return tomorrow, there would be no white bread for the Sabbath. Twenty-degree cold in the stable. The younger children were dressed only in shirts. The bird, at least, had feathers! The oldest were grouped, not around a stove, but around a book. The mother's laments did not tear them away from their study. In order to shiver less from the cold, they shivered with holiness over the Talmud. At the tap of a finger, one of them raised his curly head. While his eyes stared at me, his lips continued to munch the holy words. Ignoring my apparition, he stuck his nose again into his Hebrew. An old man, standing in front of the window, chanted over another Talmud. The cold, the hunger, the dimming light, the invasion of three strangers, nothing disturbs a Jew in contact with God. The human supplications of the woman clashed with the extraterrestrial voices of the children and the old man.

We entered twenty of these huts. Everywhere, children in shirt-sleeves, readers of Talmud, women in tears, inspired beards and those wild fruits with just skin on their bones. And the smell? The smell of a moldy corpse, macerated in onion juice. And the atmosphere? None of the huts had a chimney. They were like Russian *isbas*.* The smoke from the stove spreads across the tiny room, your eyes sting and your throat is sore. What famine! I discovered why the frock coats of these Jews are so threadbare – it is because they must boil them in their pots on days of great hunger!

No furniture! Three planks of wood for a bed, the wall of the *isba* constituting the fourth side. And mud in lieu of a floor.

One of our visits was more tragic than the others. The woman was lying on a pallet, four children asleep around her. The Jew, on seeing us enter, made a gesture like a blessing. He took me for the doctor, a doctor from Khust or even from heaven.

"He wants you to save his wife who is dying," said Ben.

Indeed, she had the look of death. Since I did not move, the Jew dragged me by the sleeve and led me to the bed.

"Pretend," said Ben, "it will be an act of mercy."

---

*   Log huts.

I could never have imagined such a scene. The children and the sick woman were rotting on this dung heap. I began to hallucinate, bitterly, and my eyes wandered across the room: two nails planted on a table represented the livelihood of this family. The father was a Talmud binder. This was his workshop. In good months, he earned fifteen crowns, twelve francs!* Two other children, whom we had not yet noticed, huddled in a corner, their silhouettes framed by sidelocks, were staring with their beautiful eyes at the man who had come to save Mother!

***

We went to look at the synagogue. The Torah, the Crowned Bride, was not better lodged than its adorers. The Jews, who had not ceased to follow us, filled the poor, holy shack. All of them surrounded us. Two local burghers, a miller and the owner of a sawmill, without sidelocks and dressed in European clothes, came to greet us on behalf of the community.

"They think that you are bringing them money," they told us.

"They are all suffering from hunger," I said.

"They have always suffered from hunger."

"How is it that they don't die?"

"Israel is tough!"

"So, let them go further afield!"

"It's even worse there."

"Let them go to the cities!"

"Dressed as they are? With those clothes? Without a penny! Misery keeps them glued here."

"And Palestine?"

---

*   Twelve old French francs in 1929 would be equivalent to something less than $10 in modern United States currency.

"The Messiah has not yet come."

"Are they truly waiting for him?"

"Yes, sir, we are waiting for him!"

The conversation ended. We extinguished our cigarettes. A singer began singing a sacred verse. The ecstatic gaze of those hollow Jews rose toward the ark of the Torah. Of what import the misery of the dwelling? The treasure is up there!

CHAPTER 9

I Met the Wandering Jew

I met the Wandering Jew. He was walking in the Carpathians, a little after the village of Volkovisk. His boots had holes in them, so one could see his socks, which also had holes. A caftan, taken well in at the waist, enveloped him from the neck to his ankles. Over his black hair, a large, flat hat, from which flowed two well-tended sidelocks, completed the glorious silhouette. A piece of checked material forming two pouches – one flapping over his stomach, the other over his back – hung from his left shoulder. He walked with big strides as he made his way in the snow.

We stopped the car and walked toward him. Feeling threatened, he quickened his pace. Ben called out to him. He didn't want to know. We caught up with him. His face evinced a frightened look. It was him, Ahasuerus.* His shoes had not completely worn down in nineteen hundred years. I was overcome with emotion.

"Tell me, where are you going and where have you come from? Are you tired? Do you have any money?"

"He says that he is traveling to Novo-Selitza," said Solomon.

---

* Ahasuerus is one of the names given to the Wandering Jew. According to legend, Ahasuerus jeered at Christ as he carried the cross to Golgotha and, for this, he was cursed to wander the earth until the Second Coming.

"And then?"

"He will travel to Ganitz."

"And then?"

"He will travel to Romania."

"And then?"

"He says that he spends Yom Kippur [the Day of Atonement] every year at the home of the *tzaddik* [miracle-making rabbi]* of Vizhnitz."

"Is he all alone?"

"No, he is married with five children."

"Are his children little wandering Jews?"

"They live with their mother in his hut on the Czech-Romanian border."

"Tell him to get into the car. We shall drive him to Novo-Selitza."

"He doesn't want to."

"Why?"

"He is afraid."

"He has never been in a car?"

"Never!"

"Come with us, Wandering Jew, we won't go fast. You'll tell me your story. I am so delighted to have met you. You have a beautiful head, your eyes glow with intelligence. At last, it's you! Come, I'll give you some socks!"

We took him on board. Now, all four of us were racing across the Marmarosh Mountains. We took an inventory of his pouches. One was his storeroom and the other his pantry. In the first, a dozen pencils, three dozen candles, two pairs of scissors, a calendar and

---

* Londres's definition of *tzaddik* is not entirely correct. In Jewish tradition the term *tzaddik* refers to a man who is righteous and of outstanding piety. It was also used to refer to Hassidic rabbis.

cigarette-butt tobacco. In the second, ten onions, two frozen herrings, a piece of white bread folded in paper (Sabbath bread) and a small pile of wild plums.

He had left his hut nine days ago, traveling from Jewish village to Jewish village. He told us that he had set out on the basis of false information, believing that alms from America had arrived in the region. First, he would have had his share, then he would have liquidated his bazaar. But he continued anyhow. Was he not a good Jew? What sin against the Eternal could he be reproached of? Did his prayers not ascend every day to His throne? Was it possible for the Lord not to watch over him?

He was born in Cluj, in Transylvania. The pogroms of 1927 had driven him away. Beaten up by Romanian students, his house burned down, the Torah defiled in the public square, he had fled. In Cluj, he had worked as a merchant in the markets. Now…

I should stress, here, how marvelous it was for me to have the Wandering Jew in my automobile. It was truly "him." Before the invention of photography, I would not have dared make such an affirmation with so much assurance. You would have rebuked me for being too fanciful or for pulling the wool over your eyes. But here he is. You can see him just as I do. I caught him red-handed, despite himself, off-guard, in the village of Ganitz in the Marmarosh Mountains, on the southern slope of the Carpathians, this winter, in the bitter cold, close to wolves.

His name was Schwartzbard, like that of Adv. Henri Torres's client who gunned down Symon Petliura, on rue Racine in Paris, because Petliura had presided over the massacre of 150,000 Jews in 1919 in the Ukrainian steppes.

When I noticed the eternal Jew on the snow slopes, I did not think that he was selling pencils and candles but that he was walking toward Jerusalem. I told him so. He immediately took me for a *chalutz,* a pioneer, a laborer of Palestine – meaning, a nonbeliever, a denigrator of prophecies. He answered that he loved and feared God. I returned to the issue of Jerusalem. He answered that the time had not yet come. I asked him from where he derived his certitude. He answered, "From the *tzaddik.*" And from where did the *tzaddik* derive his? He answered that the *tzaddik* of Vizhnitz spoke to God as well as to the prophet Elijah and that, when the time of the return came, one or the other would certainly let it be known to the *tzaddik.*

Ben and Solomon railed against these wonder rabbis. They insisted that the rabbis were responsible for all this darkness. "Do you know that from the Marmarosh Mountains to Galicia, from Transylvania to Bessarabia, from Bukovina to Ukraine, from Warsaw to Vilna, there are more than six million living in this physical and moral plight? Look, this is what these rabbis have done to the Jews."

Solitary, no longer sporting even a caftan, covered in rags, hand-me-downs from big cities, or in old shawls like old ladies, Jews descended the slopes of the mountain frozen to the bone, holding little parcels under their arms or in their hands. What are they doing? Where are they going? Why are they always on the road? The Ruthenians stand around their homes. Not for them the vagabond's bundle or the pilgrim's staff. Rooted, they grow above their roots. The Jews have their roots on their heads. These roots escape from the mane of hair under their hats and bonnets. Is this why they hang on to heaven rather than to earth?

"Where are you going?"

We had stopped one of the shawl wearers. He, like the others, spoke only Yiddish. He was going to the neighboring village. For what purpose? To sleep there. And then? He would travel to Khust. For what purpose? To sleep there. Then he would travel to

Mukachevo to see Rabbi Zangwitch and ask him to pray for two of his businesses. What does he do? No profession!

I wanted to know if Rabbi Zangwitch was a wonder rabbi.

"Not even!" said Ben as he wiped the ice off an indignant sole.

"Hey!" Solomon called out to another.

This one was older. With his sleeves serving as a muff, his little parcel hung from one of his wrists and flapped on his stomach.

"Where are you going?"

"I am leaving the village," he answered.

"Why?"

"There is nothing left to eat."

"What do you do?"

"I teach religion."

"Go to the cities, to Kosice for example. You'll find pupils."

"I am prohibited because of my dress. When police officers see us, they say, 'What are you doing here? Return to your homes.'"

"So you don't know where you are traveling to?"

"I shall ask the advice of the rabbi of Bushtyna."

What better for a countryside than to be populated by peasants? But this countryside was haunted by inspired figures. We met – or so it seemed – real students whose studies had been interrupted solely by poverty. They had the heads of old philosophers, of young poets, of accursed but conscious visionaries.

Distress was articulated only through the tongues of the women. In each village, these pitiful women surrounded the car. They tugged at our clothes and, tears flowing, uttered litanies of misfortune. We had to visit each one of their *stubes*.* They showed us the open roofs, the mud inside, their four, five or six children shivering with cold, the dried plums in the container, the grandfather dressed in rags and

---

*   *Shtub* means "home" in Yiddish.

moaning over the stove, the little girls who did not grow because of deprivation, the idiots laughing on the dung heap, the babies dressed in shirts, *barefoot on the ice.*

The mothers parted their shawls to show us their milkless breasts and fleshless ribs. The husband of one of the women had tried twice to go down to the cities to earn bread, twice he fell on the way, exhausted. He was dumb with despair. The smell in the shacks was *unbearable.* I was only able to stand it by digging my teeth into my handkerchief. And people say, rich as a Rothschild!*

In the last ten years, the misery here has increased tenfold. Before the latest peace treaties, these Jews would go away every year and work for three months on the rich Hungarian plain. The frontier separates the plain from the mountain. Today the Hungarians refuse to grant passports to their former subjects, now Czech. Three months of work was enough for these Jews to live on for the rest of the year. Now, the entire year depends on the meager fruits from the trees of the Carpathian Mountains!

"Do you want to learn about the power of the rabbis?" Ben leads me to the edge of a village. A hut is lost in the snow. We push the door open. The place is empty. The man we are seeking must be walking like all the others. But here is his story: He killed his brother. The Czech courts judged him legally. He served three years in prison, after which he returned to the village. There, the justice of the rabbi reigned. In front of the community, gathered together in the synagogue, the culprit was declared a pariah. This was five years ago. No one speaks to him anymore. When Jews meet him, they turn away. Ben says that he looks like a dog poking his head out at passersby in the hope they will take off his muzzle.

---

*   Londres is referring to the common misconception according to which all Jews were wealthy.

***

The Wandering Jew was not an enemy of the motor vehicle. He did not get out of the car once. In Ternovo, where we stopped for four hours, he remained in his seat for four hours.

"Ben, ask him what he can sell in these parts," I requested. "No one has a cent."

"He says that a good Jew is not obliged to sell, but he is obliged to stop on Friday at the first star and never offend God," Ben responded.

Ah! The holy Marmarosh Mountains!

We reached Ganitz. Solomon and Ben assured me that we had to visit the notary. A notary? The environs hardly justified such a term. They showed me a plaque on the only building that resembled a house. A notary in the Marmarosh Mountains? The sight of a fisherman watching his bait trembling in a barrel of smoked herring would have surprised me less.

The man who received us cut a fine figure. He sported sidelocks and a beard, but his sidelocks were discreet and his beard disciplined. He was dressed in black, but like a man rather than a beggar. His face was pale but his body was solid. He was certainly the only man in these mountains whose safe box did not ring empty. A notary? Yes and no. He had been one in Bratislava. Then, one day, he had crossed the Marmarosh Mountains. His Jewish heart had melted. He was certainly not rich enough to dispel this region of its misery, but he would devote himself to making it less wild. Since then, he lived here. He received alms from American aid organizations and distributed them. I found myself facing the Saint Vincent de Paul of the Carpathian Mountains: Mr. Rosenfeld.

"Come see," he said to me, as he threw an animal skin over his back. "It's the most indescribable misery!"

"I've seen it," I said.

He assured me that I had not seen everything. We went out. He showed me a shack like the other shacks.

"How many people do you think live inside?"

"Three."

"Seventeen, constituting three families. Go in!"

Thirteen were present. Three beds! But it was clear that these beds were just repugnant kennels. No Western dog would deign to spend an hour on them. Children swarmed like a litter of puppies. The women clung to Rosenfeld, uttering harrowing cries of misery. They said that the cold and hunger was unbearable.

"These wretched souls love me a lot," said the notary. "But if I gave them one of my arms, they would boil and eat it, their hunger is so great!"

We left this human kennel. Rosenfeld pointed to the whole mountain.

"It's everywhere the same," he said, "and even worse! There are more than 120,000 in this condition! And nothing can be done! Nothing! They can't leave, they only speak Yiddish and you well know that language is the real frontier!"

***

We left the Wandering Jew at Novo-Selitza. Previously, at our request, he had taken out his fortune from the pocket of his caftan: one crown and forty, meaning five cents in gold, exactly! Now he was climbing an entirely white mountainside. I watched him for a long time. His back bent, his double horse pouch over his meager shoulder, solitary, he resumed his journey, loving and fearing God.

CHAPTER 10

The Specter

Now, a specter is barring our way. He is not white, he is red. He roams over Transylvania, over Bessarabia, over Ukraine. Without him, we would not understand the worried gaze of the Jews from this part of Europe, their fearful comportment, their bent backs, their love of dead-end alleys, nor why, when out in the street, they hug walls and speak in hushed voices, nor their furtive, vigilant curiosity. At the slightest occurrence, they react like a criminal who hears a knock on the door. Indeed, all of them, in these countries, feel they are guilty of a crime: that of being Jewish.

The specter is called pogrom.

He is not terribly old. Until the Chmielnicki massacres,* Jews were mainly beaten up rather than murdered. The modern pogrom was born in Russia, in the reign of Alexander III, in the year 1881.

His character was not clear at first. His name was not notorious. He strolled around, in his youth, with the tranquility of a stranger. The earth was not as small as it is today. One did not hear, sitting by one's fire, the voice of the world booming out of a mahogany box.

---

* The name derives from Cossack leader Bogdan Chmielnicki, who instigated the murder of tens of thousands of Jews in Ukraine in the period 1648–1649.

The dead had long been buried when the smell of a pogrom crossed frontiers.

A pogrom is a form of rabies. It does not affect animals, only men, particularly soldiers and students. How does it spread? It is believed to be passed on by governments. Governments that look to the West are not affected by this virus. Those that look to the East have it in their veins.

The rabid do not bite everyone. Their teeth dig only into Jews. The sight of a caftan, a beard and sidelocks electrifies them. Pogroms have their own dates as well as wars. The first ones occurred in 1881–1882. They began with a tally of seven hundred. A pogrom is like a forest fire: the first tree that goes up in smoke sets all the others alight. In one stroke, this pogrom spread across twenty-eight provinces of old Russia. Then we come to 1903, to the first pogrom that bears a name: the Kishinev pogrom (Bessarabia). Then 1905.* Then the great pogrom of 1918–1920 in Ukraine and eastern Galicia. Then, December 1927 in Romania.

First, three statistics to put you better in the picture:

More than one hundred fifty thousand killed.

More than three hundred thousand wounded.

More than one million beaten and pillaged, just in Ukraine and Galicia in 1918–1919.

If we study them closely, we see that pogroms present themselves in three forms: non-bloody, bloody, and cruel and sadistic.

***

That of December 4, 1927, in Romania was a non-bloody form of pogrom.

---

*   Odessa.

Ever since new treaties allotted Romania territories inhabited by Jews, Romania's intellectual youth has bubbled over with anti-Semitism. From 1922 to 1927, the students did not let one year pass without making their views known: attacking the Jewish students' house in Transylvania; sacking synagogues, Jewish newspaper offices and cemeteries; throwing Jews out of trains; smashing the windows and signposts of Jewish houses. And, at the end of 1926, the assassination in Cernauti of the Jewish student Falik by the Romanian student Totu. Motive: one was Romanian, the other a Jew!

In December 1927, Romanian university students decide to hold their congress in the city of Oradea-Mare (Transylvania). Oradea-Mare is inhabited by Jews. The agenda of the congress: war against the Jews.

A general, a former minister and a renowned doctor open the proceedings and incite the students.

The blood of youth runs fast. The students do not wait until they are in the street. They have, in the hall, a Jew at hand: Alexander Flescher, a journalist who is doing his job at the press table. It is a stroke of luck. They beat him to death.

Then they take to the streets. They number five thousand. In groups of twenty-five to thirty, they invade the town. Jews found on trams are thrown out, onto the ground, as the trams roll on. Every passerby – even without the clothing or the beard but with just a hint of Israel in the face – is beaten. They visit cafés and restaurants and boot out non-Christian customers. Teams armed with hammers and clubs smash the windows of Jewish stores. Lodged in the homes of residents, that is of Jews, they eject their hosts from their homes. Finally, the stampede against the synagogues. Everything is smashed with axes. They grab the holy books and the "crowned brides." They tear them up, defile them and carry them triumphantly to public squares, where they set them ablaze, dancing around the fire and blessing the flames. The police and mounted guards watch over the saturnalia.

After the congress ends, the students stop in Cluj, in Ciuca, in Huedin, in Targu Ocna. Everywhere the party begins again. This is what is called a moderate pogrom. Long live Romania!

***

In the second form of pogrom, they kill and they lynch. Let us take the years 1918–1919. In Kiev, Ukrainian soldiers stop Jews in the street, rob them and shoot them. In the course of ten days, soldiers from the Black Sea camp at Bobriuskaya station, those from Petliura's regiment at Sorny station, Ukrainian Cossacks at Fostov, Post-Volynsky, Romoday, Kazatin, Dachnay, Bakhmach stations… Jews found in carriages are stripped, beaten and killed. At Bakhmach, the platforms are covered in blood.

On January 4, 1919, the death company lands in Berdichev. Jews found at the station are killed. The company reaches the city. The old are lashed with riding crops. Uncertainty prevails when facing children; the Jewish type is not always very pronounced. The companions of death ask: "Yid or not?" The Jew is shot. Houses are stormed. Jews are led into the street, forced to cry "Death to Yids!" and shot.

From Berdichev, the companions move on to Zhitomir. Same ritual. From Zhitomir, they attack Ovruch. The ataman,* Kozyr Zyrko, summons the Jews to the station. The Cossacks escort them with lashes of *nagaika*s and make them sing "Majofes,"† the holy Sabbath hymn. The procession arrives in sight of the station; Kozyr

---

* Term for a Cossack leader.

† "Mah yafis."

Zyrko orders his men to fire, into the singing and into the flesh. And long live Kozyr Zyrko!

***

Blood is a bad alcohol for savages. Not all savages live in Africa or in the Pacific. In order to be a savage, you do not have to be naked. Ours, the European savages, the Ukrainian soldiers, wore boots, uniforms and medals.

We arrive at the cruel, sadistic form.

In Ovruch, nothing much. The Jews are ordered to whip each other, then the instigator of the whipping is forced to kiss the bruised spot. But let us move on to Proskurov. Until now, the killings were followed by pillaging. Peasants, who did not take part in the blood feast, would often rush with baskets and sacks at the sound of the massacres to harvest the remains left by the Cossacks. The Proskurov affair assumes a sacred character. The killing is not going to be a prelude to pillaging. They are going to kill not for profit but out of duty. The ataman Semossenko makes his companions swear, on their flag: hands soaked in blood but clean!

So the company, *a musical band at its head and ambulance in tow, sets out*. It crosses Proskurov, arrives at the ghetto and begins its work. The purity of its intentions requires it to operate with blank cartridges. In groups of fifteen or so men, they enter the houses – from the stores to the upper floors, without wasting time in stairwells – and run their bayonets through every Jew they come across. The Cossacks only fire when a Jew manages to escape. Everything is ransacked, even the cradles. To those who offer money to ward off death, they answer: "We only want your life." A priest, crucifix in hand, emerges from a church and entreats them, in the name of Christ, to stop the massacre. They kill the priest. Children are bound to the still-warm bodies of their fathers. When it comes to raping, they jumble mothers and daughters together with the same fury. Fifteen hundred killed between three and six o'clock in the afternoon.

In Felshtin, Shargorod and Peschanka, the Cossacks are even more Cossack. They cut off tongues and gouge eyes. They force mothers to hold out their children to them and decapitate the little victims. They undress the men, make them hold hands, order them to sing and dance, then: "Fire!"

In Bratslav, Jews are hung by their hands, their flesh sliced with sabers. The pieces that fall, they cook. They play ball with the heads.

The mothers offered themselves to save their children. The Cossacks answered: "Yid chicks must be killed in the egg." And they disemboweled the angels! Men, women and children were bound to the tails of horses. They shaved the males and, before executing them, made them eat their beards. A father, on all fours, was forced to lick the blood of his son. A rabbi, pointing to seventy children, cried out to the Cossacks: "You killed their fathers and their mothers; now, what am I to do with them?"

"Shoot them all!" was the reply. And long live the ataman!

Why these pogroms? Why did the Turks kill the Armenians? Why does a cat scratch the eyes out of a dog? Because race speaks louder than humanity. A Hebrew always sticks in the throat of a Slav. And a long life together has not brought them closer. A Pole or a Russian chases a Jew from a pavement as though the Jew, who is passing by, is stealing his air. A Jew, in the eyes of an eastern European, is the incarnation of a parasite.

Calamities have causes. Elsewhere, one seeks the cause with clear independence of mind. Here, whatever the calamity, the first cause that comes to mind is the Jew. And how ironic when one thinks that it was the Jews who invented the scapegoat. Their priests endowed this creature with their sins and drove it away. The nations of the East retained the idea. But they replaced the goat with the Jew!

The fundamental cause of pogroms is loathing of Jews.

Then come the pretexts. They are numerous. In the case of the Ukrainian pogroms, the pretext was Bolshevism. Petliura's Cossacks were anti-Bolshevik, and the Jews, according to the rules of the game and from time immemorial, had to be Bolshevik.

Note the different tone. Let us take, for example, this order signed by Semossenko and posted in Proskurov, on the eve of the massacres:

> I urge the population to stop its anarchic demonstrations. I draw the attention of the Yids to this. Know that you are a people who are detested by every nation. You sow trouble among Christian people. Do you not want to live? And do you not have pity on your nation? If we leave you in peace, so live in peace. Miserable people, you do not cease to instill disquiet in the minds of the poor Ukrainian people.

And if hail destroys the harvests, it is also, you can be sure, the fault of Israel!

This is what it means to be Jewish in the countries we have visited.

CHAPTER 11

The Meiselmann Family

Solomon returned to the Marmarosh Mountains.

Ginger-headed Ben preferred to follow me. He has relatives almost everywhere – in Transylvania, Bukovina, Bessarabia and Warsaw. I pointed out the rules of propriety which oblige every man to pay regular visits to his family. Ben understood.

It was not the first time that I broached the issue of how Jewish kinship traverses frontiers. My pocket contained letters from English Jews to cousins in Berlin, Warsaw and even Constantinople. When he adopts European dress, the Jew of the East adopts Europe and America!

We reached Oradea-Mare. When the trains begin to follow the snow instead of timetables, they lose touch with dates. Ours had lost twenty hours as it engaged in this winter sport. Thoughtlessly, it deposited us in Transylvania at five in the morning.

It deposited no one else, since there were just the two of us. Trains do not always find madmen to put in their compartments! And to think that the people we are coming to see hail from a hot country!

On the horizon were neither Jews, nor Romanians, nor horses, nor sleighs – only a light above the exit door and, to welcome us, a thermometer registering minus twenty-nine degrees. We were cool!

Ben was not acquainted with Oradea-Mare any more than I. We did not even know on which side the city lay. "If your relatives are dead," I said to Ben, "which after all is quite possible, for what godly reason have we come to this glacier?"

"In this age," answered Ben, "wherever Jews live, they live on a glacier." I immediately understood better why Theodor Herzl wanted to send them to Palestine.

"Stand straight," I said to Ben. "The cold makes you hunch-backed, and your silhouette frightens me on such a dark night and in such snow!" The cold had nothing to do with the hump: Ben, like all good Jews, carried a mysterious little packet. No longer able to hold it in his hand, he had put it on his back, under his overcoat, which was wrapped tightly around him.

Nonetheless, we proceeded on our way. Walking assures a man that he has not yet turned into a stalactite. "Find me a job in France," Ben said, interrupting the white silence. "I speak thirteen languages, and here it is so cold that I can't even open my mouth!"

"What would you like to do?"

"Warm myself in the Paris sun."

"I will recommend you to a travel agency as a Mont Blanc guide! Do you have any brothers, Ben?"

"I have one who is registered as a Pole and another who is doing well in New York. I don't know whether he will become American."

"Why are you in the Carpathians?"

"Because of President Masaryk, who gave us our freedom."

"Do you know where we are going?"

"Yes, I can feel the sled tracks in the snow."

The two of us were a sight! Particularly the companion with the hump on his back. Two pale revelers on the lookout for the first car. Ah! Not all Jews live on place de la Bourse!

***

A day that had begun so well could only get worse. Indeed, daylight had hardly broken when we committed a theft. Oradea-Mare was asleep. On the door of every Jewish house, on street doors as on apartment doors, a long, fingerlike cylinder in zinc or copper was screwed at an angle into the wood. The cylinder is called a *mezuzah*. I had seen it in London, in Prague, in the Marmarosh Mountains. I had asked a hundred times what it contained and only received a vague answer: "A prayer." Ben gave me the same answer.

"Let's unscrew one and you'll read to me what it contains," I suggested. Ben protested. I pointed out to him that we would be committing only a violation of common law, not sacrilege. At this price, I was authorized to become a criminal. Anyway, it was agreed that we would replace the cylinder at nightfall. So I removed the zinc finger.

What is more useful to travelers than hotelkeepers? I hold them in utmost veneration. If one could recognize them in the street, I would take my hat off to all of them. Ring the bell anywhere, at six in the morning, and you would normally have insults hurled at you from the window. Had these fallen on us icemen, they would have certainly broken a rib or two.

The Transylvanian hotelkeeper graciously opened his house to us. But he must have been an alcoholic – for morning coffee, he brought us a bowl of brandied peaches! We sat down at a table.

The cylinder contained a piece of paper that had been folded twenty times. I unraveled the paper; it revealed Hebrew script. It was the first breakfast of which I had partaken accompanied by Hebrew and brandied peaches! This is what Ben translated:

Hear O Israel, the Lord our God, the Lord is one. May
His great name be blessed forever and for all eternity.

Thou shalt love the Lord, your God, with all thy heart,
with all thy soul and with all thy might. And these words
which I command thee this day shall be in thine heart.
And thou shalt teach them diligently to thy children and
thou shalt talk of them when thou sittest in thy house
and when thou walkest by the way, and when thou liest
down and when thou risest up. And thou shalt bind them
for a sign upon thine arm and they shall be as frontlets
between thine eyes. And thou shalt write them upon the
posts of thy house and on thy gates. That thy days may be
multiplied and the days of thy children in the land which
the Lord swore unto thy fathers to give them, as the days
of heaven upon the earth.”*

"Do all *mezuzah*s say the same thing?" I inquired.

"All of them!" answered Ben, no doubt fearing that I was about
to go and unscrew another one!

At noon, we called for a coachman. Two arrived. We took the
one who seemed the most able. The other shouted a rude remark at
him, but without anger and more in irony. The two were Jews and
spoke Yiddish. The unlucky one snarled at the other: "Rascal! You
are Romanian and you don't speak Romanian!"

We set out to look for the Meiselmann family. The shop signs
were the same as in Whitechapel. The stores looked like branches of
those in London. For a painter, the Jews of this region are no match
for the Jews of the Marmarosh Mountains. The sidelocks are rarer,
the caftans not obligatory and the beards more civilized. But they

---

*   Deuteronomy 6:4–9; 11:21.

still cannot be taken for Romanian: the hair, eyes, complexion and manners belong to another race. Misery is no longer obligatory: these are very small shop owners who, in the era of coin money, would have lived on bronze coins rather than silver ones.

Ben tapped the back of the coachman. We got out of the sled. Ben had found his family. "Go in!" he told me. The shop sign read *Galanterie* (chivalry). Some business! Ben explained to me that his relatives, who had come from Little Poland, had forgotten the right word. They had wanted to write *Galanteria*, meaning "haberdashery." Too bad!

Let us enter the chivalry store anyway.

The Jewish stores, barely the size of a car, operate on the same principle as big department stores. They sell everything, and more old stuff than new. The Meiselmann family seemed to me to be all there, for I counted seven heads – more than the number of customers in one day. The Meiselmanns, although delighted, appeared worried. Ben said, "See the state of their minds: they want to know if some calamity has happened!"

The pogrom had come to the area some fourteen months ago. It still lived in the memory of all of them. Meiselmann the father, Meiselmann the mother, Meiselmann progeny spoke of nothing else to Ben. I followed the conversation through their fingers and facial expressions. Miming and gesticulating, the Meiselmanns acted out all the emotions their souls had undergone. First fear – they held their breath; then anguish – their eyes opened wide; then fright – their hands froze in mid-motion, as though petrified. Then panic: the father got up and ran frantically to the store's narrow recess. Then, a moment of calm, the pogromic wave seemed to wane. Motionless, the Meiselmanns listened. Suddenly, the sound of shattering glass: the mother's fist, pounding a metal plate against the wall, recreates the hammer blows through the windows. It's the students bursting into the store. The oldest son opens the back door and reenacts the flight of his two sisters. The mother bars this escape door with her body, and two sons position themselves in front of her. Now the mother's fingers count the number of assailants: two times ten! But fear has big eyes; twenty students could never have fit into the little store. The father is belted with a riding crop – *ouch*! Here in the neck! There on the left shoulder blade! The entire store is overturned, shoes trampling over caps, clocks smashed. Not a single drawer left in place, a veritable earthquake!

In the afternoon the same story was retold in over twenty stores, where Meiselmann introduced his cousin Ben. It seemed as though the tidal wave had occurred yesterday – no doubt because they fear it will return tomorrow. The Bucharest government does not understand that the Jews, not being Romanian, are unable to live, act or think like Romanians. A state and a nation are two different things. The Jews want to be part of the Romanian state, but can they be part of the Romanian nation? It is not, they say, within their power. What a problem! Even after the blows, they still feel Jewish!

***

It was Friday. The Sabbath was about to begin. In all the streets, the shutters fell with nightfall. The Jews were returning home to don their festive clothes. I followed Ben to the Meiselmann home. We waited in the closed store. Father and son came down in their finest attire. Sadly, they did not have a Sabbath hat of rabbit tails. They were each carrying a prayer book under an arm. We went out. The streets were filled with Jews on their way to synagogue. New holy Torah scrolls had replaced those that had been damaged and burned in 1927. We entered a synagogue. The rabbi, standing on a dais, was already reciting verses from the Torah. Four other Jews standing around the rabbi were following, each in turn, with profound devotion, the portion of the day of the Holy Book.[*] Faith transported the congregation to another realm. How far they were, at that moment, from the students, the pogroms and Romania!

Then each one returned to his home, and Ben to the home of the Meiselmanns. Could I leave Ben?

I was invited to the Sabbath dinner.

The interior of the Galanterie was unrecognizable. The broom and feather duster had done their work. Order had replaced disorder. A shining white tablecloth covered the table. Two napkins were laid over something. A five-branched candelabrum held five candles. The mother blessed the candles and lit them. The family stood, waiting for the father's arrival. Meiselmann appeared. He raised the two napkins, under which lay two white loaves. With a priestly gesture, he blessed the loaves and cut them into slices. He passed around the slices and everyone dipped his in a bowl of salt. The father recited another prayer in Hebrew. Then we sat down.[†]

Jewish families are not sparing on Friday nights and Saturdays. The custom is to eat a lot and drink wine to the glory of the Lord. They served stuffed carp, bloodless meat and a mountain of weirdly shaped cakes. The father apologized for not having any more wine from Palestine. There was a shortage in Oradea-Mare. Everyone seemed very joyful. The concern for their safety temporarily lay dormant in the hearts of these souls, grouped, that night, at the foot of the throne of the Eternal, their King. When the cakes arrived, the

---

[*]   The portion of the Torah is actually read on Saturday morning, not Friday evening as Londres represents.

[†]   Londres has the order of the Sabbath evening slightly garbled. Candles would have been lit earlier in the evening before sunset. Kiddush, the blessing over the wine, would have preceded rather than followed the blessing over the bread.

father launched into a melody, one of those Oriental chants that tug at one's heart like a departing ship.

Ben and I got up. But the family remained seated at table and, from each mouth, another chant emerged. Then all of them, as though propelled by an intense inner flame, began to dance on the spot. It was the famous "Majofes"; God was singing through the mouths of His subjects. He was saying: "How beautiful you are, how sweet you are in your contentment, when you speak to Me and I listen, oh My people!"

In Lithuania, Ukraine, Bessarabia, Bukovina, Galicia and the Marmarosh Mountains, every week, on the same day, at the same hour, Israel – whether it is Polish, Russian, Romanian, Hungarian or Czechoslovakian – is no longer scattered but united.

CHAPTER 12

The Pioneer from Palestine

"Shalom!"

"Shalom!"

Ben and another man hugged each other at the Kishinev station. This done, they engaged in conversation. You should have seen them! Their fingers danced like puppets. When you say that a person blushes, you think of his cheeks. When a Jew blushes, he must blush under his nails, his hands play such a big part in the expression of his feelings.

We have arrived in Bessarabia.

The man who welcomes us is clearly very different from all the other Jews in these countries. His chest is not slumped; he stands straight, with proud shoulders. As he crosses the streets, he does not cast his eyes warily in every direction or quicken his steps. He wears a cap. He is dressed in a leather jacket and, when he puts his hands in his pockets, one senses that, for him, a stranger is not a ghost who augurs catastrophe.

He is a *chalutz*, a pioneer from Palestine.

We reach the town.

The signs above the stores bear the same names as those in Whitechapel, Mukachevo and Oradea-Mare.

The pioneer has a mission. He arrived here two months ago and will return to Jerusalem in three months. He has come to bring news about the homeland.

One day, the world awoke to see Young Turks overthrowing tradition; I am now looking at the first Young Jew!

I convey to him my surprise and tell him that his appearance represents a real breach in the Jewish front.

"There are 160,000 like me!" he answers proudly.

We walk on. He leads us to his house.

"I used to have sidelocks, my dear sir! I was brought up in a *yeshiva* [Jewish religious school]."

We arrive at the house of Zionism. Above his bed hangs a portrait of Theodor Herzl.

The pioneer takes out of his pocket a slim, well-bound notebook and places it under Ben's nose. He turns it over to show him the two sides. It is a passport. Frontiers may move again, but he will never again be a Russian subject, nor Polish, nor Romanian, nor Hungarian, even though Herzl was one! He is now a citizen, a citizen of Palestine.

"A Jewish citizen," he clarifies, as though to chase away the last shadow of doubt from our minds. "And you," he says to Ben, "you are still a subject, a slave?"

Ben defends himself. He is Jewish, one of the 180,000 Jews of Czechoslovakia who have declared themselves Jews.

"You are a Jew through charity. You live under the flag of another nation."

"And on top of that he wants to come and live in Paris rather than Jerusalem!" I say.

The pioneer gave him a big, friendly slap on his shoulder. Then he opened a case.

Photos! Albums! A small blue-and-white flag, and a song entitled "Hatikvah."

"It means *hope*," said Ben.

It was their national anthem:

As long as in the heart within,
A Jewish soul still yearns,
And onward, toward the ends of the east,
An eye still looks toward Zion,

Our hope is not yet lost,
The ancient hope
To return to the land of our fathers,
The city where David encamped.

As long as tears from our eyes,
Flow like benevolent rain....

As long as the waters of the Jordan
In fullness swell its banks,
And to the Sea of Galilee
With tumultuous noise fall....

As long as the beloved walls
Appear before our eyes....

As long as pure tears flow
Before the ruins of the Temple....

Hear, O my brothers in the lands of exile
The voice of one of our visionaries,
Only from the very last Jew
Will die our last hope.*

———————————————

*   This is a longer version of the current national anthem of Israel, based on the original poem by Naftali Herz Imber.

Ben's emotion was palpable. His eyes glazed over for a moment. He read the hymn again in Hebrew. Then he placed the sheet devoutly on the table.

"This is the flag," said Alter Fischer, the pioneer.

As we examined it, he continued: "It hangs from the balconies of Tel Aviv on holidays. It is placed at the head of processions, on top of our town hall and on top of our schools. I heard a cry arise and I can still feel it here" – he touches his heart – "an unbelievable cry, a cry that you never heard, nor millions of others, a cry that has not been heard for twenty centuries: Long live the Jews!"

Ben instinctively looked around him.

"There we can open our windows when we say this, while you…! 'Long live the Jews,' sir, for someone who only ever heard 'Death to the Jews!' – this represents a revolution of the soul. Even miracle-making rabbis who see the prophet Elijah descend would not experience such emotion."

Alter Fischer was twenty-eight years old. He did not just burn with the fire of Zionism, he seemed to be cradled also by the waters of the Sea of Galilee. He smiled at the new man he represented. Lovingly, he opened an album.

"Look, what was here in 1910? Sand dunes. And here, what do you see today? A huge city. A city has replaced the sand dunes, that's all, and it is Tel Aviv! Here is Herzl Street, Rothschild Boulevard, Max Nordau Street, the high school, the town hall, the casino, the synagogue whose dome can be seen from the sea, rising above everything! We are building a theater that is going to be magnificent. We have a beautiful country!"

"What have you come to do here, Mr. Fischer?"

"I have come to show these things to the young. Israel has created a miracle, a miracle that can be seen and touched. I am one of the

voices of this miracle. There should be Palestinian Jews in every corner of the world where Jews are groaning."

Alter Fischer, the pioneer, was not born in Bessarabia, but in
Ukraine. In 1919, he was eighteen years old.

"I lived in Zhitomir…"

In the history of pogroms, Zhitomir is illustrious.

"I saw everything. They forgot to kill me, that is why I am here.
Meaning that two Cossacks tried to skewer me but four Jews, fleeing from a house, loomed in front of them. They lost time assassi-
nating them. I ran toward the cemetery. Luckily, I did not remain
there. Later, they massacred all those who had taken refuge in the
mortuary.

"At the time, I was a Jewish fowl. Chickens and ducks are
allowed to roam around farms; then, one fine day, they are caught
and slaughtered in broad daylight. The blood that is shed leaves no
stains on anyone. The operation is legal. In Palestine, I was taught,
first of all, to stand straight. Stand straight, Ben!"

Bessarabia is a nest of Jews. Czarist Russia, in its horror of Jews,
had driven the chosen people to the edge of the country. Thus, as a
result of treaty games, a large number of Jews found themselves cut
off from Russia. They are today Lithuanians, Poles and Romanians.
But they are still steeped in Russian sauce, speaking Yiddish but
also Russian and sporting short, Russian-style boots. They mill
about in relative tranquility in the streets of Kishinev. Their modest
businesses do modestly well… In short, herring and onions did not
seem to me to be in short supply.

Alter Fischer did his work passionately. In the afternoon we
accompanied him to the home of a rabbi who, like all rabbis, put a
spoke in his nationalistic project. Bessarabia has given birth to many
Zionists. The pure, the Orthodox, are therefore quite concerned.
The rabbi received us courteously. He wore a grayish semi-top hat

that was too small. But such intellectual Jewish figures can get away with what would seem ridiculous on the head of a sophisticated dancer! The conversation took place in Hebrew. This is what I understood:

In order to express himself, the pioneer began with a tone of respect. On hearing the name Tel Aviv, the rabbi, stroking his beard with his fingers, shook his head; on hearing the name Jerusalem, he raised his eyes to heaven. The pioneer opened his album, spread the panorama of the new Jewish capital before the eyes of the holy man, and laid his forefinger on the dome of the synagogue. The rabbi then opened his mouth. He seemed to say: "It's nothing to boast about – that there is only one synagogue in your Tel Aviv." The pioneer turned the pages and tried to find, in every picture of a settlement, the temple of the Torah. The rabbi began to comb his beard with his other hand.

The pioneer asked him politely to read "Hatikvah." The rabbi took his glasses but did not place them around his ears, preferring to hold the instrument with two fingers. He read attentively till the end and returned the paper to the pioneer, emotionless, undoubtedly thinking that a nation that possesses the law of Moses does not need trombones, bugles and drums. The pioneer accompanied his words with the most restrained gestures. The utterance of the name of Theodor Herzl seemed catastrophic to me. The rabbi forced a smile but his face quickly resumed its gravity. Then the pioneer cited names, names of pious Jews certainly. Then he invoked other rabbis: Rebbe Aaron, Rebbe Keppler, Rebbe Siovits. Then one could discern that he was describing a Yom Kippur service in the Jezreel Valley. The rabbi remained amiable throughout but, toward the end, he hardly paid attention to the worthy pioneer's presentation. His eyes were raised, no doubt, toward distant Sinai! We left the rabbi's home.

Alter Fischer was furious. He led us through Kishinev with great gusto. It warmed us up.

"Whoever put the idea of the Messiah into their heads?" he asked. As though he had forgotten that he himself had once been a yeshiva student. "By dint of waiting for him, they will all end up slaughtered. They are like the inhabitants of Stromboli, waiting for the volcano to erupt!"

"Mr. Fischer, you number fourteen million, of whom more than half live on volcanoes that are more or less dormant; you cannot all go and live in Palestine."

"Live, no – but belong, yes. We can issue millions of passports, like mine."

"Governments will burn your passports in public places."

"I want to see the day!"

"Indeed, we shall see this later, Mr. Fischer. But for the moment, let us go and dine. The stomach calls!"

My table that night was a veritable compass rose indicating every direction of Israel, but only to the East: a Jew from Little Russia, two Polish Jews, a Romanian Jew, a Czech Jew, a Lithuanian Jew, a Hungarian Jew and a Jew: Alter Fischer. So many ideas in the air! So active are the minds of these Jews! Only a people who never stopped searching can be tempted by an insoluble problem. We covered everything: Lord Balfour, Theodor Herzl, the idea of a Jewish bank.

"You know," said the Jew from Little Russia, "a Jewish bank is not something fanciful. If it wanted to…!"

We spoke about rabbis, and about European politics.

"We are a multinational people," said Ben the Czech. "One day, Europe too will be multinational. And multinational does not mean less national. When Europe becomes multinational, the Jewish question will disappear."

They talked about Zionist leaders, the Arabs…

"We want to get along with the Arabs," said the pioneer. "But if *they* don't want to, we'll make ourselves understood."

England's agenda was explored in depth.

"It is using you," said Ben, "and when you are no longer useful, it will abandon you."

No one argued with that.

And they did not forget the assimilated Jews, the Jews of the West, particularly, the French Jews – "the most selfish of all." Sirs! You have been defamed!

CHAPTER 13

Do You Want to
Go to Jerusalem?

Czernowitz is the capital of Bukovina. But since Bukovina became part of Romania, Czernowitz is known today as Cernauti. It is a city perched high. One can reach it more quickly by plane than by train, not because a plane is faster but because of the position of the city, which is closer to heaven than to earth.

It is a city that is not afraid. Lost in the middle of landlocked lands, it takes itself for a seaport. You need to plant your feet firmly in your shoes if you wish to avoid tripping at the spectacle it offers. It is Hamburg without the Elbe, or Marseille without the sea. Cernauti has no water, not even a drop, but every shipping company in the world has offices here.

The first one I came across was Lloyd Sabaudo. Two enormous ocean liners on each side of the signboard invited travelers to undertake long trips. At first, I thought that Lloyd Sabaudo was a little mad or else that its signboard was the result of some kind of vow, a commemorative plaque by shipwreck survivors. I continued on my way and passed by a Jew whom I mistook for a Moldovan peasant. Then I noticed on the first floor of a building:

Norddeutscher-Lloyd-Bremen-Amerika. So many survivors in this country! Further on: Hambourg-Amerika Linie. I was on the verge of stopping a resident to ask him for an explanation, but the signs kept converging on me. Back-to-back came Cunard Line and Canadian Pacific. If you wanted to see a man amazed, you should have seen me there, at that moment. These were not commemorative plaques: the offices were open below, handsome offices, *birou di voïag,** with everything needed to send a man to the end of the earth. Then, painted above Atlantic waves, three enormous letters: NGI – Navigazione Generale Italiana. I was already quite overwhelmed by the time I reached the Royal Mail Line, further down the road. I walked along, thinking that France was altogether more coherent. You do not set up shipping companies on the summit of a mountain with a view only of glaciers. Common sense, I told myself, is truly the supreme quality of the French. We may lack certain gifts, but we have balanced minds.

"Hey!" said Ben. He had been listening to my monologue without a squeak, but now he pointed with his finger: "La Transat, French company, Brazil, Argentina, Uruguay."

In order to respond to such provocation, all that was left to do was to decamp immediately and fly a banner in the middle of the Pacific in the name of the Bernese, Lepontine and Bergamasque Alps!

To top it all, the *birou di voïag* were not idle. Crowds waited outside their doors, in the cold, like aficionados of *Manon* lining up on the pavement of the Opéra-Comique.[†] These future travelers were mountaineers, badly encased in sheepskin jackets but well topped

---

*   Romanian for "*bureau de voyage*" (travel agency).

†   *Manon* is a popular opera by the French composer Jules Massenet (1842–1912). The Opéra-Comique is a noted opera company in Paris.

with pointed hats of imitation astrakhan. Viewed from behind, they looked like members of the Ku Klux Klan. Ruthenians, Little Russians, Moldavians, they dreamed patiently in front of the magical posters – some of Canada, others of Argentina. Good business does not live solely on wealth; misery created these *birou di voïag*. Fields that yield no profit filled the boats.

In front of the Atlantic, a Jew stood chewing his moustache, wistfully contemplated the happy emigrants. He looked like one of those beggars who sniff around the lingering aromas of a kitchen. Ben asked him if he was also leaving. With a sad movement of the hand, the Jew dismissed this beautiful hope. But he did not stir. He had the facial expression of Charlie Chaplin watching a circus disappear into the horizon.

***

Out of Cernauti's one hundred forty thousand inhabitants, eighty thousand are Jews. Out of one hundred shopkeepers, ninety-two are Jews. Above the doors appear the same names as those found in Whitechapel, Prague, Oradea-Mare and Kishinev: Goldenberg, Landau, Wolf, Nathan, Salomon, Jacob and some local names, ending in *ich* and *weiz*, which have not yet crossed the continent. We walked down Regina-Maria Street. Jewish shopkeepers hang their bait on the street. Little jackets, hats, shoes, shorts and gloves are suspended on iron rods. The streets look like the aisles of an imaginary closet whose clothes, aided by the wind, wave their fleas over passersby.

You are not watching two men on the path of adventure. We are clearly cognizant, Ben and I, of where our feet are taking us: they are leading us to the Sassners. The Sassners are not friends of ours; they have never heard of us and we only first heard of them an hour ago.

But I asked Ben to be very polite and introduce me as a very refined person so that they will not show us the door.

The Sassners recently returned from Palestine. They are going to play, for the first time in front of us, the part of disillusioned Zionists.

Here is their shop. Mrs. Sassner, whom I see from the street, is cold. She is bundled in a shawl which clearly does not warm her. She sells herrings and buns topped with poppy seeds. Before their adventure, the Sassners owned a real shop, on Regina-Maria, and sold furs. From otter skins to herring skins, what a downfall!

At first, Mrs. Sassner appeared crestfallen: we were clearly not buyers. But Ben quickly cajoled her with Sabbath Yiddish.

"She told me," he said, "not to go there."

"That's not what you should ask her. First, why did she go there – she, her sister, her husband and their two children?"

"She says that it was her husband's decision because he is enlightened. She says that all the young people are also enlightened and that those who put Palestine into their heads should get a beating."

"Where did they settle?"

"In Tel Aviv."

"If they were selling furs, then I understand."

"No! They became *frysers.** She, the children, her sister, the husband, all cut hair and beards, but there were soon as many *frysers* as there were beards. And they were not the only ones to leave. More left, she says, than came. She says that Palestine is good for the very rich or the very poor, those who have nothing to lose and those who no longer need to earn."

"Ask her what became of their vision."

"She says... But you have understood," said Ben.

---

*   The Yiddish word for hairdresser is פריזירער or *frizirer*.

Indeed, she pointed with her hand to her herrings: her husband's vision had floundered in brine!

The male Sassner appeared. He did not share his spouse's bitterness. Palestine had worked against him, but he was not against Palestine. He defended rather well the idea that victory is won primarily by the dead and the wounded.

"Ask him if he knew that Zionism is founded on agriculture and not on commerce."

The former Tel Aviv hairdresser was cognizant of this. But his faith had lacked the strength to make him till the land. He had wanted to champion Zionism on the cheap. He concluded that the Sassners' return proved nothing against Theodor Herzl. A Jewish wife is respectfully submissive toward her husband, so Mrs. Sassner refrained from shrugging her shoulders.

From there, the two accomplices, meaning the two of us, left for other stores.

"We shall go in," I said to Ben, "and you will ask point-blank: 'Do you want to go to Palestine?'"

We entered the store of Jacob Isler, a signboard painter. He was completing in blue letters the commission of a certain Mr. Samuel Mandula. Leaning over the signboard, it seemed as if, in order to work faster, he was painting one letter with his paintbrush and another with his beard. Ben went straight to the point.

Jacob Isler got up and said nothing at first. He cast an anxious look at the street, fearing, no doubt, that we had come with reinforcements.

Then he asked, "What organization do you belong to?"

"Our aim is to know how many immigrants Cernauti can provide."

"Is this for the Romanian government?"

"No, it's an internal Jewish matter."

Jacob Isler said that he was happy here.

"But you have the portrait of Theodor Herzl on your wall."

"It's not forbidden!" he protested.

"So, you do not want to go to Palestine?"

"No! I am too old."

We left.

From the door of his workshop, paintbrush in hand, Jacob Isler followed the mysterious ambassadors with his eyes for a long time.

Next was Mr. Bela Polak, the bookseller. We entered.

"Shalom!" said Ben.

"Shalom!"

We leafed through an old Talmud. I even purchased the *Zohar*, the book of splendor. The bookseller took us for kabbalists. He was one, too. God wanted to be loved with joy, with ecstasy, through wine, dancing and singing, not through asceticism. We assured him that we were of the same opinion. Together we derided the Gaon of Vilna, who had cursed this beautiful book, and I nudged Ben with my elbow. He proceeded to fire our question.

The bookseller shook his head and fanned his chest with his beard. He said that the Jewish question was not in the hands of men. One could, of course, go to Palestine, but the sign had not yet been given. The ingathering of Israel had not yet been proclaimed. He was going to stay in Cernauti. It was not too difficult to earn enough for the white bread of the Sabbath. As for spiritual persecutions, the soul of a Jew was sufficiently acquainted with their taste not to be surprised by them.

We left.

Juda Fried worked as a watchmaker. We could see him, from the pavement, head bent over his bench, fiddling with the hairspring of a lady's watch. It was minus twenty-six degrees outside. Attracted by the indoors, we pushed Juda Fried's door.

Theodor Herzl's portrait hung in the middle of the clocks.

"Shalom!" the watchmaker greeted us.

"Shalom!"

Having constant trouble with my watch, I naturally placed it in the hands of the expert. And I asked Ben to tell him to do a good job, as I was due to undertake a long voyage. I was going to Jerusalem.

At the mention of Jerusalem, a second worker, a young man, looked up and spoke to Ben. The father joined in the conversation. Juda Fried explained that Zionism had turned his son's head and it was he who had bought Herzl's portrait.

"Tell him that I'll take his son with me, if he wants."

A whiff of anger sent a tremor through the beard of the chief watchmaker. His son would never go there, never!

"And when he is older?"

"Then he'll have other ideas!"

Juda Fried did not look at us amicably. He took us for *chalutzim*. He would certainly sabotage my watch.

***

In the store of a horsemeat sausage vendor, we met Mr. Salomon R——, an old man seated next to a stove. On hearing French, he got up and said, "Greetings, sirs!"

Salomon R—— was clean-shaven and miserably dressed. Poverty and philosophy accompanied him with dignity. He told us that meeting us in this isolated country made him happy because he had lived for a long time in France.

Zadoc Kahn was a friend of his father, who had been chief rabbi of Frankfurt. He himself had lived in Paris like a true Frenchman, and then for a long time in Vienna. He was finishing his days in Cernauti – the Jewish community having come to his rescue, in memory of his family's history. He declared, "I greet you warmly, and my thanks to France for its legendary hospitality! I have had a long life, sirs, seventy-three years. But I was never French, nor German, nor Romanian – always Jewish!"

"Then perhaps you can still go to Palestine?"

"Sirs, I spent seventy-three years charming Europeans. Let others charm the Arabs!"

CHAPTER 14

The Lwow Ghetto

"My anger will not persist eternally…"*

But, Lord, it persists in Lwow, against Your daughter Israel.

A new side of Jewish life faces us. We have just crossed another frontier. We are now in Poland, in Little Poland, "Mala Polska." In Galicia.

Under the Austrians, the city was called Lemberg. Now it is called Lwow. In French it is also known as Leopol.

We are going to see the first ghetto.

In Czechoslovakia and in Romania, we caught a glimpse of Jewish centers. But there was no demarcation line between the Jews and the Europeans, just a mixed population where the Jews were dominant. In Lwow the Jews are separate. They number eighty thousand against two hundred thousand Poles. If one accords to the word *against* its full meaning, it would be more correct to say that two hundred thousand Poles are against eighty thousand Jews.

The life they live here is infernal. They all want to flee. Twenty thousand left in 1926, fifteen thousand in 1927. But the United States and Canada have just closed their doors to them. Argentina

---

* Jeremiah 3:12.

demands one hundred fifty dollars. France makes it difficult. Palestine tempts only the young. The nightmare goes on.

Polish Lwow is a pretty city. But we have come to see the other Lwow. It is at the very end of Legions Avenue behind the grand theater, which marks the border. The hotel porter smiled at first when I asked him the way to the ghetto. Then he said, "It's straight ahead, you'll see it, go on."

"To what desolation have you been reduced? To what horrible confusion! Your dwellings have been cast down."* It is of the Lwow ghetto, no doubt, that Jeremiah was speaking.

The houses were destroyed in 1918, at the time of the last serious pogrom. The sons of Israel, walking vultures, wander day and night in the alleyways, as though searching for scraps. Their hands wrapped in pieces of cloth, black against the snow, heads hunched into their shoulders by the mallet of misery, thoughtful, idle, standing still for no reason, in the middle of squares like prophets without a voice and without listeners, they afforest this ghetto rather than animate it, with their tormented, cypress-like silhouettes.

The doors, the walls of their makeshift stores, are barricaded by advertising billboards. Placed like bandages on the wounds of their domiciles, these sheets of tin or cardboard impart a harlequin look to their houses. The neighborhood is steeped in the smell of onion and herring. One herring – that is saying a lot; more like one herring divided into six! The pieces, spread out on a newspaper, tempt the starving owner of ten *grosze*.† Pretzels, little breads glazed with egg and sprinkled with poppy seeds, rival the herring squares. The

---

*   Jeremiah 9:19 (9:18 in Jewish Bibles). Londres has switched the verse's first-person "we" and "our" to the second-person "you" and "your."

†   A grosz, one-hundredth of a złoty, was approximately equivalent to the value of a cent today.

entire ghetto eats standing up. One only has the right to sit at table on Friday night. They eat walking, as though rushing to urgent business. One man buys his pretzel, bites into it, and notices that other long teeth have already gnawed at his goods. He returns it and takes another. What is left of this little bread for the next passerby?

The market is the heart of the ghetto. A pile of shacks like those built after an earthquake or fire. But the earthquake or fire must have taken place long ago.

These shacks are shaking. Life, however, resides therein! If manna is going to fall, it will fall here.

"*Handel, handel!* For sale!" all the Jews cry out. For sale! I am trading, I sell everything! I sell old stuff, naturally, but is not the old as worthy as the new? A soul simply has to be beautiful, pure, intact to serve as a mirror for the Lord. Do beautiful clothes make a beautiful soul? Does the Lord look at your shoes, your caftans? Here are stockings, socks that no longer have feet. But do stockings need feet if your feet are already encased in shoes? *Handel!* I am selling greasy caftans, this way you can say that it was you who dirtied them in the course of a memorable feast!

"*Co pan kupujé?*" (What would you like to buy from me, mister?). One is tempted to answer: "Two pennies of misery!" It is so abundant that for two pennies one would get enough for the rest of one's life. The pretzel vendors shiver in front of their baskets and do not stop shouting, "*Pientch grosze!*" (Five cents!). And they give you their word of honor that the merchandise cost them more.

The women are fat, however. Is it because they are wrapped in rags? Does the cold make them swell? Do they suck, when their husbands are not watching, the bone of a pickled herring? Fat but pale. Their fat is like mutton fat, good for suet.

A market? A field of manure, yes! A selection from all the rubbish bins of this Polish city! The rabbits, whose skins are on offer, appear to have been slaughtered with a machine gun. The furs are nothing more than a mass of hair.

"We aren't selling anything," say the beggars.

Why do they follow us like pigeons waiting for their seeds? Is it because we don't have holes in our trousers? That would, indeed, be highly original here!

"Sirs," I tell them, "you should go to Palestine."

"Huh! There are enough of those dirty, frizzy-haired, flea-ridden, ragamuffin Jews there as it is!"

"Are you any different?"

"No, that's why. But there, you have to work hard to earn money."

"And here?"

"Here, we wait and we don't come down with malaria."

"What are you waiting for?"

"For an overcoat and a detachable collar, like yours."

"And then?"

Many hands answer for all. The gesture is well known; it means that these men are the children of the Lord and that the God of Israel is a powerful being.

***

The streets were nothing to speak of. The Lwow ghetto is indoors. We spent three days visiting it. If we were to give you an account of our work, we would have to take the streets one by one and, beginning at number 1, draw up a list such as this:

Synagogue Street:

No. 1: nine families of five to eight children, crying of cold and hunger and rotting on the foulest of dung heaps.
No. 2: ten families, ditto.

No. 3, no. 4, on both sides of the street, all the way down,
ditto.
Ditto for the sloping streets, flat streets, dead-end streets.
The day before yesterday, from two to six o'clock, yesterday from nine to twelve, today from one to seven, ditto.

On the first day, I had to rush out from one of these doghouses in
order to overcome the nausea caused by the smell. For the same
reason, I had to rush out on the second day and twice on the third
day. The two Jews who accompanied me cried and, in the evening,
they sat at my table but were unable to eat.

On Slonecznej Street (Street of the sun), we step into a basement.
My companions light candles and we grope our way in. No sound
of a voice, and yet thirty-two people live in these subterranean lodgings. We push the first door. What are we penetrating into? We
trudge in mud. An anemic light filters through a vent blocked with
snow. The humidity has enveloped us with its veil and we feel the
veil slowly sticking to our bodies. We scour the den aided by our
candles. Two little children, aged three and four, hands and feet
wrapped in rags but dressed in shirts, their hair having certainly
never been combed since it had the misfortune of growing on their
heads, stand shivering by a pallet. The pallet seems to stir. We lower
our candles. A woman is lying there. But in what is she lying? In wet
shavings? In stable straw? I touch it; it is cold and sticky. What is
covering the woman would once have been a quilt, but is now nothing more than a mush of feathers and cloth oozing damp like a wall.
We notice two more heads in the mush, tiny tots, four months,
fifteen months old. The oldest smiles at the flame, which we wave
above them.

The woman did not utter a word.

We awakened this underground world. Residents encircle us in the corridor. We have to enter each den. If they are indoors in the afternoon, it is because they do not have clothes to go outside with. One resident had gone out for all of them, wearing the shoes of one man and the caftan of another. Will he bring back a little something to eat?

Wrapped in a shawl, a Jew with a long beard greets us in the dark. He used to own a house but it was burned down in the pogrom of 1918 and, if he is lame, it is because he was thrown out of the first-floor window. Since then, he has been unable to work his way up again. He lives in the basement.

We clutch our handkerchiefs over our noses with our teeth. The Jews show us the reason for the terrible stench. The neighborhood's main sewer passes through their home, through the homes of everyone on this street; more than three thousand Jews have been transformed into sewage cleaners, for it was not mud in which we were trudging.

The women cling to us, emit howls of misery and let themselves be dragged as we climb up the stairs. Outside, in the street, their cheeks glistening with tears, their lips supplicating, they pitch their shirt-clad children in front of us, like a barrier.

"Don't give them anything," my companions tell me. "One would need trainloads of zlotys to quench their misery. It renders them stupid, blind, hunchbacked. The children rot. Don't give anything, nothing."

***

So, what to do?

Nothing. It's the ghetto, that's all. Resignation will long continue in lieu of a solution.

This tragic misery is to some extent their doing, their creation. Not specifically that of the Jews of today, but of the Jews of always. A Jew wants to be independent. To this end, he chooses the role of vendor. He sells! He would raise fleas to sell their skins if the skins of fleas were in demand! Can a city with 95 percent vendors survive?

Undoubtedly, Poland hates them. It drove them from all state companies, it expelled them from its national life, even more so than did the Czars. But Poland rejected only those who did not wish to assimilate. Poland does not wish to be more Jewish than the Jews are Polish. And as Poland is the stronger, the Jews cry under its weight. They are crushed, muzzled, covered in dung, but do you think they ask for mercy? Listen closely: they are moaning. What are they saying? They are saying that they are Jewish! Piłsudski* cannot cede his place to Moses!

I was standing on the pavement of Smoczej Street (Street of the dragon), taking notes. A Pole passes by, carrying a bucket of water. He digs his elbow into my ribs and shouts: "*Przecz ž drogi psie przcklenty!*"

"Hey, what's going on?" I ask.

"It's nothing," say my companions, "don't make a fuss. He saw you with us and took you for a Jew."

"What did he say?"

"He said: 'Piss off, out of my way, you dirty dog!'"

---

*   Józef Piłsudski (1867-1935), prime minister of Poland at the time and de facto leader of the Second Polish Republic.

CHAPTER 15

In Contrast…Warsaw!

Hello to the Jewish capital of Europe! And sorry, Poles – your metropolis is also that of Israel!

We are now in Warsaw. We saw the wild Jews of the Marmarosh Mountains; the frightened Jews of Transylvania, of Bessarabia and of Bukovina; the begging, beaten Jews of Lwow.

Here, there are no more sidelocks. They lost them to the scissors of the Cossacks, who were ordered by the Czars to cut them off in the street.

Is not Whitechapel a thriving Jewish center? Yes! But too European. Vilna, Lodz, Cracow? Great Jewish centers certainly. Amazing visions! Entire lives unbeknown to Westerners. A people, thousands of years old, living below telephone wires and next to railway lines! But Warsaw is the Jewish queen of Europe. If Saul, David, Solomon, Rehoboam, Jeroboam and Nadab had a successor, the king of the Jews would have his throne in Warsaw.

He would have more subjects in New York, but what kind of subjects! Ungodly people ready to sell the Ark of the Covenant, if they could find it. But in Warsaw, David II would be on home ground.

It would be a pretty little capital: three hundred sixty thousand descendants of Abraham. True, he would have difficulty recognizing them initially. Europe marred a good number of them. He would have to blow the *shofar** in Catholic neighborhoods to obtain a general gathering. But it would not take him long.

I can visualize him, this David II, making his entry into Nalewki.† He would have first spent the night in the Polish center, at the Bristol Hotel, for example. The following morning, after a good night's rest, he would have gotten into a tank, if he wanted to enter his kingdom alive. Five minutes later, he would make his entry into Nalewki, proclaiming: "I bring you peace! I have come to make a sacrifice to the Lord; purify yourselves and come with me!"

Immediately, streaming out from Smotcha, Dzika, Gesia, Stawki, Mila, Pokorna, Maranowska, Pawia, Zoliborska Streets, emerging from underground caves and corridors, still unexplored by Gentiles, tumbling down ancient rickety stairs, leaping from passageways, alleys, and dead-end streets, springing from squares, running from markets, abandoning stores, rushing out of houses of prayer, prayer shawls still on their heads and phylacteries on their foreheads and arms, three hundred sixty thousand caftans, sporting short boots and flat hats, beards flying, waving their hands like flowers, would have streamed down Nalewki, crying, "*Yechi hamelech!* Long live King David II!"

I saw this dream, when I was fully awake, today. I was there, in this amazing ghetto, constantly pushed from my spot by Jews rushing from one place to another. They darted around, undisciplined, possessed by a frenetic demon that was neutralized from the start. As they passed by, some addressed me and, at my silence,

---

* A ram's horn, whose call is considered a spiritual awakening in Jewish tradition.

† Nalewki was a street name in the Warsaw ghetto and was used to refer to the entire ghetto area.

resumed their course. They had said, "Please, sir, do you want some merchandise?"

The Polish government had forbidden their participation in Polish activities. It had closed all the doors to them as employees. Driven away from railways, trams, post offices and salt mines, only one Jewish postman had remained, of late, in the employment of the state. The minister when questioned said that he had dismissed him because Jews are not good walkers. Did you hear that, Wandering Jew? Station porters had Jewish porters expelled. The last major strike in Lodz was launched by Polish socialist workers because their bosses – Jews – had taken on Jewish workers. Barred on all sides, they had converged on Nalewki.

One of the main pillars of Poland's political program is to "crush" the Jews. And the nation's maxim is: *Poles only!* The president of the republic is their president and not that of the Jews. Piłsudski tried to do something about it and persuade Poles to uphold the terms of the constitution, which are not anti-Semitic. He was unsuccessful. Jews number three and a half million in Poland. The total population is more than thirty million. The three and a half million Jews pay 40 percent of the nation's taxes and, out of a budget of more than three billion zlotys, a bone of only one hundred thousand zlotys is thrown to Israel. A Jew cannot work for the government, or the army, or a university. Just as the Jewish people are barred from jobs, Jewish workers are barred from factories, and Jewish intellectuals from top positions.

Why is this? Because the Polish government is helpless when it comes to resolving Jewish issues, so intense is the Polish ancestral hatred of the Jews. The Jews of Poland have returned to their darkest hours of captivity.

***

In spite of this, the Jews have not changed their lifestyle. A crab will dig his claws even more firmly into a rock if you try to catch him. And if the sound of a mouse gnawing drives you crazy, in the end you will get used to it. The Orthodox Jews, who are called national Jews in Warsaw, have not changed their practices in the face of their new tragedy and continue to distinguish themselves from other citizens by their flat hats and frock coats, like the yellow badge of the Middle Ages. As for the Jews with the detachable collars, whom David II would have to round up in central neighborhoods, they want to be like Western Jews, meaning Jewish only by religion. And even if they say, "We want to separate ourselves from those dirty, mangy Jews and from those rabbis who do nothing but sleep, and only be accountable to the Polish authorities," it is to no avail, for the Poles will not allow them to do so. So they came to terms with this and, when one encounters them, they exclaim, "Of course, we are foreigners!"

For the time being, they are all trying to offer as little wool as possible to the shear clippers of the Polish tax offices. I asked one of them, in Dzika Street, "Why do you not want me to photograph you?"

"I am afraid of paying taxes," he answered mischievously.

"But, you are rich!"

"When a Jew is rich, he is no longer a Jew!"

Since they are foreigners and the Polish budget allocates them no more than a hundred thousand zlotys, not even enough to collect their garbage, how are they to organize their national life? They have a small government which is called the Community. The Warsaw Community is headed by a triumvirate: an Orthodox Jew, a socialist Jew and a Zionist Jew. The Community levies Jewish taxes. It is with this money that they run their hospitals, old-age homes, schools and cemeteries.

Their commerce operates for no more than four and a half days a week because of their holy Sabbath. The Polish government does not prevent them from closing on Friday night or on Saturday but forces them to close on Sundays.

"So how on earth can we get rich?"

"Become Poles and don't keep the Sabbath."

"Never! We do not want to renounce our culture. We deeply believe in it."

And, in the streets, newspaper vendors cry out in Yiddish.

Chinese streets are no more magnificent than the streets of Zion-Warsaw. Friends of mine, who tremble at the slightest thing, prevented me from buying a folding chair which I would have like to set up, with me ensconced in it, in Nalewki. So I was exhausted, every night, when I returned to the well-heeled neighborhoods. Jews live outdoors. Since they come from the Orient, they live like Orientals. In summer, it is even better. Life is laid out entirely on the pavements. Everything, except for making children, takes place outdoors. But the winter is also good. These eternal wanderers travel far from their homes. They scurry, happy at the fact of possessing feet, and the splashing mud endows their steps with added charge.

In this ghetto, where they know everything, everything interests them. How beautiful it is to look at life! Who knows whether the cholera carousel that permanently operates at the end of Zoliborska Street does not harbor some treasure this afternoon? And there they are, rummaging even in the disinfectant machines! One of them pulls out a pair of trousers and, using his caftan as a screen, tries them on! Leaning against shacks, hopeful customers take off their shoes and try on old pairs of shoes. I could not fathom why, since the shoes they took off were no more worn than those they were purchasing. It must be from love of bartering! Tomorrow, others will acquire what these people abandon today.

The nooks and crannies of Nalewki have not all been explored, even by the police. You enter them with tremor and delight, but it is not the tremor of fear. Jews never play around with knives or guns. It is the tremor of the unknown. Dead ends, passageways inside houses, inner courtyards interconnecting with other inner courtyards, well-hidden open markets, the endless pockets of this market, of those courtyards, those passageways, those dead-end alleyways – this Oriental labyrinth is as much reminiscent of India as of Damascus and Jerusalem.

Those caravanserai without camels, those Rudyard Kipling khans – rowdy, gesticulating, carnival-like, where all the names of Israel dance on store signs; where the blind prophet gropes on his path; where motionless old people, necks tucked into their chests, resemble herons asleep on one leg; and where others slowly, slowly seem to follow an invisible procession; those entrances to stairwells that serve also as stores; those cellars from where voices cry out, "*Handel, handel!*" (For sale, for sale!); those streams in which all the Levis, Lews, Lewises, Lewites, Levitans, Lewistons and Lewinsteins, so troubled by my presence, wade around; all those gazes where worry dispels curiosity and curiosity dispels worry; those prehistoric horses whose skeletons still pull tottering removal carts; those yeshiva students, framed by their learned sidelocks and hunting, in their round hats, for an elusive dinner; those pretty girls dressed in rags under their shawls, a sachet of earth from the Holy Land around their necks, who will soon follow the trader from Buenos Aires;* those porters carrying their loads Turkish style; that humidity seeping through the walls, penetrating one's bones; those endless bright

---

*   Reference to Jewish white slave traders from Argentina who lured women from the shtetls of Eastern Europe.

eyes, shining like stars, in the midst of this immense rag-and-bone city: this is Nalewki!

***

On Friday night, at sunset, the great Sabbath curtain descends over this metropolis, the curtain that separates the people of God from the Christian dog. Everything is deserted. Only a few oafs hang around trying to sell their oranges or pretzels.

"Go home. You no longer have the right to be selling, it's Shabbat."

But they stick their tongues out at you. Nalewki has become a desert. The Jewish people are finally at home. The woman prepares the Sabbath table, brings out the white tablecloth and places candles in the seven-branched candelabrum. The man dresses in his best clothes. And, suddenly, the streets come alive again. The men, books under their arms, holding their sons' hands, make their way to the synagogues and houses of prayer. Houses of prayer are as numerous in Nalewki as bathhouses in Japan and bars in France!

There is one at no. 4 Twarda Street. I paced up and down in the passageway leading to it. The Jews began to arrive, already steeped in a devotional stance. Yet they took the time to examine me. One even stopped his holy recitation to walk around the troubling stranger that I was. His piercing eyes penetrated the secret of my pocket.

"You can come in," he said to me in French, as though he had read my passport through my overcoat.

I followed him. The door had hardly closed, I already felt suffocated by gusts of devout incantations. Standing facing Jerusalem, the Jews prayed. I could see their backs. A white prayer shawl with black stripes, the *tallit*, fell from their heads down to their hips.[*] It

---

[*]   Londres describes a morning service: prayer shawls are not worn at evening services.

is said that God appeared thus to Moses. Their long-flowing beards, peeking out from the shawls, shook in the distant direction of their destroyed Temple. The prayers slowly turned into a roar. Under the divine emotion, their bodies seemed to sway like empty boats on a stormy sea. Suddenly, I opened my eyes even wider. These men, who now stood in profile, seemed to have transformed into unicorns. A horn appeared to have grown on each forehead! It was one of those boxes that contain prayers, while the other was tied to each left arm, pressed close to the heart.* Thus the prayers declaimed by their lips entered magically into their hearts and into their brains.

This was no longer the age of Piłsudski!

And when the Lord saw that he turned aside to see, God called unto him out of the midst of the bush and said, "Moses! Moses!"

And he said, "Here am I!"†

Tonight, Polish trams, you can ring your bells across Nalewki. Israel is no longer there!

---

* *Tefillin* (phylacteries), the boxes of which Londres speaks, are not permitted to be worn on the Sabbath. They are worn only during weekday morning services, not in the evening. It is possible Londres attended a weekday morning service, which he describes, not realizing that the evening and Sabbath services differ from the service he attended.

† Exodus 3:4.

CHAPTER 16

The Rabbi Factory

Ulica Sto-Jerska 18. This is it. A typical Nalewki street – muddy, gesticulating, filled with chatter, but also mysterious. A building, humid like all the others, with its pox-dotted stones and plaster, its courtyard interconnecting with another courtyard, its sticky staircase.

They are waiting for me. Now that I have reached the first floor, all I need to do is touch the *mezuzah* with two fingers, bring my fingers to my lips and push the door.

I stand at the threshold of the Mesivta, the great seminary of world Jewry. Luminary youth, those who beg for their bread and bed in Nalewki, thin, pale-looking intellectuals in round hats, aged sixteen to twenty-two, ascetic, inspired, devoured by the spirit of Moloch,* bearers of the fire of Israel, hailing from Poland, Romania, Ukraine, Czechoslovakia and even Belgium – they are all there. I can hear them from the landing. The sound of their voices swells, falls, dies and revives. The rabbi factory is in full swing.

---

* Moloch was a Canaanite god associated with child sacrifice. Londres appears to use the term metaphorically as an entity that demands a costly sacrifice.

Let us enter. Yes, enter! The smell is terrible? Did you ever experience such smells? Pretend you have a cold, put your handkerchief over your nose and push forward. You'll get used to it!

The smell is particularly Jewish – Orthodox Jewish. In a Cernauti cinema, it drove me out before the end of the film. The smell is a mixture of essence of onion, essence of salted herring and essence of caftan fumes, admitting that a caftan can give off fumes like the coat of a sweat-drenched horse. Individually, perhaps, you do not give off a smell, I hope, but bunched together in a small space, you are lethal, sirs!

How trivial my thoughts are! What does smell have to do with this place? The five senses and even the others never penetrated a *mesivta*. Nothing from outside has an impact on these students. Absolutely nothing! They are not here to eat, sleep, touch, hear, see, taste or feel, but to learn. The passion for learning is uniquely Jewish. The sole preoccupations of these indefatigable theoreticians are to reveal mysteries, drive shadows away, stretch an intelligence that never gallops fast enough, attain a summit of comprehension only to leap across to another summit and hypothesize on every possible cause and principle.

This rabbinical seminary is extraordinary, one of those sights that engrave themselves in your memory forever. You stand there, dumbfounded, silent, as though taken aback by the unexpected. There were five hundred eighty-seven intoxicated, completely intoxicated, zealots in five rooms. Since seven o'clock they had not ceased to imbibe – to imbibe knowledge, wisdom and new discoveries. Hands on their foreheads, trudging through the Talmud with their noses, raising their starstruck eyes at times, their round hats perked at a slant, sidelocks swinging frenetically back and forth, right to left, so entranced were they with their studies they could not stay still and, with ever-increasing voices, roared like deaf soothsayers, oblivious to their neighbors. They looked like an assembly of child prophets sitting on a stack of inspiration!

They study sixteen to seventeen hours a day like this. What do they learn? First, the Talmud by heart, even two Talmuds – that of Jerusalem and that of Babylon. They literally gorge themselves on all the ancient rabbinic traditions. What is the Talmud? It is a book of interpretations of the Mosaic law, formulated by a thousand rabbis over thousands of years. It is the love of argumentation pushed to the point of insanity. The meanings and counter-meanings of a word are the object of endless arguments.

For example: You do not lightly discuss a commandment of God, such as, "Abide ye every man in his place, let no man go out of his place on the seventh day."* You ask: What is this place? How far can one go on a Sabbath without offending the Lord? Does the word *place* refer to the immediate environs of a house? Can the entire village be considered as the place meant by the Almighty? If so, does this apply to all villages, whatever their size? And then, what is the maximum perimeter of a village in order to fulfill the divine commandment? And is what is permitted for a village also applicable to a city? And where does a city begin? Where does it end? Once its boundaries have been set, is a city too big to be considered a place? If it is too big, by how much should it be reduced in order to allow walking on the Sabbath without contravening the commandment of the Almighty? And who can prove that the boundaries set for a city in order to make it accord with the definition of a place are the appropriate boundaries?

Oh, insatiable spirit of Israel!

Not only do our intoxicated students imbibe these sublime arguments, they add to them. They reject the rulings of the ancient

---

*   Exodus 16:29.

sages. They enter into unspeakable fits of anger at one old beard's conjectures.

Then they go into raptures over the subtle thinking of another. No matter how clear the sky may be, it is always a little dark in the eyes of a Hebrew. Truth is never woven sufficiently finely for a Jew. And what these young acrobats of the mind, these cerebral zealots, are learning here is not just literature and Jewish ethics but how to become sharper, more astute, more penetrating and faster. Not a bad sport!

They stay seven years in this mental furnace, studying to the point of exhaustion, aberration and, one can even say without exaggeration, hallucination. I watched the older ones, those from the fifth and sixth years: I watched them, but they did not see me. I could stand in front of a student, as though I wished to talk to him, but he was blind to my presence! Possessed by his subject, ablaze inside, transfixed by knowledge, he would get up from his bench, not to welcome me, but to exclaim and announce the genesis of a new idea.

It was not at all ridiculous but very beautiful, moving, imbued with majesty and as respectable as madness.

The material lives of these students are no less impressive than their spiritual lives. They come from the ghettos of the Carpathians, Galicia and Ukraine, and the garment they wear at sixteen when they arrive is the same as that which they wear at twenty-three when they leave. But, nonetheless, they grow and their growth can be measured by the length of the sleeves of their caftans. Fortunately, none of them have gotten fatter! From year to year, their caftans become too short but never too tight.

The Mesivta, which is funded by Jewish taxes and donations, serves them one meal a day, at three o'clock. It does not provide them with lodgings. So where do they live? They work as night guards in the stores of Nalewki. The storekeepers do not pay them, but give them a roof over their heads. As for the evening meal, one can see them hunting for it in the courtyards and markets. It takes the form of a pretzel, an orange, a piece of herring, or an onion. Even when faced with extreme poverty, Israel has always respected scholars. It is its luxury. For us, the remains of our tables go to our dogs. Israel does not like dogs, so the remains of its tables go to students.

The purity of their customs is legendary. They enter as angels and exit as angels. All the fire of their young days is reserved for the Talmud. They dream of it alone and, with it, they live and sleep. If the Torah is the crowned fiancée, the Talmud is the garlanded bride.

Not all of them will become rabbis but, when they leave the Mesivta, all of them will take up the profession of son-in-law. To be a son-in-law represents a position for a young Jew and, when you are a learned young Jew, this position honors the family into which you enter. The in-laws are proud to feed a pious man who will devote his life to studying. Having a son-in-law who has come out of the Warsaw Mesivta is such an honor that, fearing they may miss one, Orthodox Jews come to select them in the nest. Every week, the principle rabbi receives the visits of future fathers-in-law. Some even come from New York, for this sole purpose. It's so true, we are even expecting one today.

Here he is. He does not sport a beard or a caftan. This American is a European. It is the second meeting he is about to have with the director. He offers to deposit ten thousand dollars in advance as a dowry. The check is ready. But he hesitates over the son-in-law. The principle rabbi sings the praises of four. Of these, the American selects two. But which of the two will it be? The spiritual father of these fortunate fiancés-to-be does not want to influence the decision. Let's go see them.

We penetrate into one of the five workshops of this intellectual factory. The brains are operating full blast. The human machines take no more notice of the father-in-law and matrimonial rabbi than they did of me. They continue to sway frenetically. Will it be the fervent one, with the loud cries, who will win the unknown beautiful virgin from New York? No, the two potential fiancés are a small fellow, who holds his forehead in his hand and balances his head like a pendulum, and a taller one who, if one believes his gestures and lip movements, is engaged in a heated discussion with a Babylonian sage. Neither are plump. How fortunate that the American is rich!

The father-in-law will give his answer tomorrow. I think the smaller one will win. Since both are equally learned, is it not better to have a few centimeters less to feed?

***

At seven o'clock in the evening, the distinguished students break camp. The Talmud under their arms, they make their way in great strides toward the stores where they serve as watchdogs. A pretzel vendor, positioned at the corner of Nalewki and Dzika, offers one a pretzel as a gift. He devours it on the spot.

"Are you hungry?"

"When one wants to study, one has to suffer."

"You don't seem to eat enough," says Ben as he hands him a *chalukah.*

"My aim is not to eat, but to know."

And the student disappears into Dzika, which means *wild!*

---

* A Hebrew term for alms, which were slated primarily for the residents of the Holy Land.

CHAPTER 17

Your Purse or Your Furniture

Can one imagine finding humor in the act of following a tax inspector about to make wretched people cry?

A Polish clerk, in charge of the Jews of Nalewki, assured me that this was so, one evening in Warsaw, while it snowed and we drank some Tokay* at the late Mr. Fukiera's establishment.†

"Do not say such a thing, hard-hearted fellow," I told him. The comical side of misery only aggravates it.

The tax inspector insisted that I did not know what I was talking about. The employees of the Polish state did not receive princely salaries but those who, like him, handled the Jewish quarter did not complain. Instead of enriching themselves, they got a few good laughs.

"If you want to laugh, all you have to do is come look for me. You'll find me ready, even before noon!"

Thus, the following morning, at nine o'clock in the Warsaw ghetto, between nos. 41 and 45 ulica Gesia, a man was smacking his buttocks in order to keep awake.

---

*   Wine from the Tokaj region of Hungary.

†   This was a noted wine cellar in Warsaw, still a famous restaurant today.

It is easy to recognize the man who was thus humiliating himself: he is the martyred journeyman, the poor traveler who is not allowed a night's sleep, and whom newspaper editors send out on the road in temperatures of minus thirty-six degrees, as though he were an Eskimo!

This morning, the temperature was no higher than minus 7. We quivered with contentment. I paced up and down between nos. 41 and 45. I resembled an unarmed sentry fearlessly keeping guard. You would not believe how such behavior could create so much commotion in ulica Gesia. The Jews watched me anxiously from the doorsteps of their stores. Having observed me, for eight days, wandering, stopping, delving into their courtyards, they had become obsessed with my silhouette. What catastrophe would result from this meticulous inspection? Did I have a bomb in my pocket? If so, what type? Political? Economic? Religious? Many had followed me in order to resolve the mystery. The moment I turned around to look at them, they would also turn around, raising their heads and pretending, with an air of indifference, to follow the direction of the wind. But today I limited the field of my observations. I directed my fire at three buildings. Poor Jews of nos. 41, 43 and 45, what did you do to anger the Lord? Will peace never come to you? To you and to us? Who could say whether the mysterious stranger might not cross pavements in the afternoon? Caftans huddled against caftans. Mini war councils were held. With the bobbing of heads, their flat round hats simultaneously opened and closed the gates of fear and of hope.

My clerk had not arrived. I knew that ulica Gesia meant Goose Street. Did he take me for the godfather of the ulica?

A peasant's cart drawn by a horse that had never seen hay stood in front of no. 43. It was clear that this removal vehicle belonged to the Polish tax authorities. Armed with a fearsome briefcase, my man appeared. We shook hands. The fears of the Jews reached their peak. Under their startled gaze, we entered no. 41.

***

The government cart was a sign that the Warsaw treasury had reached the limits of intimidation. Your money or your furniture. Whoever said that it is never humid when it is freezing cold? That meteorologist never spent a winter in Nalewki. This building reeks of humidity. It is poor! It is miserable! The sun is so beautiful, over there, in Palestine!

We begin on the first floor and knock on the door. Silence. The cart driver, who has joined us, also knocks. Silence again. The tax-man then assumes a gruff voice and says something in Polish. A tiny child opens the door.

By the window, five children follow a finger as it walks across the Talmud. It is the finger of a magnificent old man. Without removing his finger, the old man gazes at us. The clerk hands him a bill of debt for thirty-three zlotys. The old man stares at it.

"You are Isaac Goldschmitt, teacher of religion?"

The clerk waves his paper as though to incite the other to take it.

"I don't know how to read Polish."

The cart driver serves also as the interpreter. He speaks to the old man in Yiddish.

"Why do I have to pay?" asks the old man. Pointing to his beard, he asks: "For this?" Then pointing to the children: "For them?"

"Where is the furniture that was here fifteen days ago?"

"It is with more fortunate individuals, honorable clerk."

"You hid them with a neighbor, as always?"

The teacher points to his Talmud and says, "See how it is worn. Fortunately, I shall die soon!"

The Pole tells the cart driver to tell the old man that he is not an undertaker's assistant but a tax inspector.

The old man pulls his beard and offers it to him.

"I should have it cut off and taken away."

"The Lord, blessed be He, the Lord will punish you, honorable clerk!"

We gave up and went to the apartment across the hall.

Surprised, two women throw shawls over their shoulders. The clerk sits on the bed to indicate that he is not in a hurry. One of the women takes the bill of debt and looks at the sky.

"Forty zlotys!" she repeats.

She goes into another room. We wait. She returns and says, "Here you are!"

She hands over five zlotys.

"Forty, madam, forty!"

She leaves again, returns and adds three zlotys.

"Forty, madam."

She sits down on the bed next to us and begins bargaining.

The clerk tells her that taxes are not herrings.

She leaves again and returns with two zlotys.

"Take away the chairs!"

Before the cart driver manages to take hold of them, the two women sit on the chairs.

"Take away the sideboard!"

Dragging the chairs, the women rush in front of the sideboard.

A man enters the room: "Mr. Clerk, ten years ago we spoke only Russian. Knowing that Poland would be happy to hear Jews speak Polish, we learned Polish. Is that not worth forty zlotys?"

"Mr. Rappoport, I am removing your furniture."

The man utters a cry of lament. The clerk and the cart driver laugh.

"What did he say?" I ask.

"He feels sorry for the horse," the cart driver explains. "He says, 'Poor Polish horse, with you, innocent creature, we shall share our misery!'"

Rappoport extracts ten zlotys from the pocket of his caftan and tells the clerk that, if he comes back in a month, he may receive more than he is demanding, for he (Rappoport) has some great business ideas and he plans, from now until then, to become richer than all the moneylenders, his compatriots who already live on Holy Cross Street.

The clerk accepts.

Second floor. Here, if my information is correct, I am about to see something new. The bill of debt is for 125 zlotys. A pretty Jewish lady gives us a warm welcome. She shows us the two-room apartment and says she is alone at home. The clerk taps the wallpaper with his hand. Rolls of paper are stuck on top of each other but the entire apparatus is not well glued to the wall. We move a piece of furniture that stands guard in front of the panel and pull out a few nails from a corner. The artificial wallpaper collapses and all one has to do is push a hidden door. We find ourselves in a small workshop where two men, seated at machines, are knitting stockings.

One of every four apartments is disguised in this way.

A Jew is thus, simultaneously, an industrialist and a trader. He manufactures at home and sells from his basket. No factory, no store, no bosses. Legally independent and prudently secretive.

One of the two men counts 125 zlotys and pays the bill of debt. Rebuked by the clerk, he retorts that his lodgings have nothing mysterious about them. He had simply walled himself in with his son to get away from the women's chatter!

The building reverberated with the presence of the tax inspector. Doors banged. Landings rumbled with the moving of furniture.

People hurtled down the stairs as though in a fox chase. Before we had reached the third floor, two women, each waving a Jewish baby at the ends of their arms, barring the landing, hurled horrifying wails in our direction. Frightened, the babies added their cries to those of their mothers.

"They say," translated the cart driver, "that their babies are pleading with you not to take their cots away."

"Do not shake your children in this manner, shrews!"

They won the day. We did not stop at their homes.

Opposite, an old man was waiting for us. His sons must certainly have been in the chase and were now dragging their anxious souls around Nalewki. The father possessed one of those pure, beautiful ghetto heads, far removed from our era, the head that Michelangelo gave to Moses, but wizened while waiting for prophecies to come true. His gaze, bare of all human preoccupations, innocently accompanied the gaze of the tax inspector as he searched the rooms. There being nothing to seize, we prepared to leave, when the Michelangelo model extended his hand to us.

"What? He's asking us for charity, now?"

"Yep," said the cart driver, "he says that one does not ask money from an old saint, one gives him money!"

We moved on to no. 45.

A grocer who sold salt and herrings – the salt being none other than that from the herring barrels, and you have an idea of what the soups taste like! – raised his arms when he noticed the clerk. He had been ordered to tear down, by today, a brick partition over the entry to a secret room. He, of course, denied the existence of a secret room. He had never heard about such a room, nor had his wife, and his father even less. If, from the time of the Russians, former residents fiddled with the lodgings, was he responsible? He would need to pay ten zlotys to have the wall broken through. Let the Polish government advance him the sum of ten zlotys and everything would be ready in fifteen days!

"Do you see how they operate? You come to collect a debt, they turn things around in such a way that you give them a loan!"

He owed forty-five zlotys to the treasury. From his door, the man called out to the Jews watching from the pavement opposite. They rushed forward, each one delving into his caftan. The collection produced eighteen zlotys. He took ten zlotys out of his drawer and, clasping his hands, uttered a plea for mercy. He asked to be exempted from the remainder, pity on his old father. One by one, he opened the drawers to show they were empty. He went to the back room, took down a portrait and brought it to us: a portrait of Piłsudski. He loved Piłsudski. His son counted in Polish and spoke it. Was not he, the father, a good citizen?

"Another seventeen zlotys, Mr. Yehuda Mond!"

He pointed to the herring barrels. "So take the rest in merchandise."

"Seventeen zlotys or I will take away the herrings!"

As the cart driver prepared to load up, Mr. Yehuda Mond drew from his pocket a bill of one hundred zlotys and, regaining his dignity, waited with the impatient air of a creditor for the tax inspector to give him his change!

Fourth floor. Seven people, including three young boys, in one big room. Mother and daughter in tears. Two Jews in caftans both slouched in chairs. The three young boys, who were reading the Talmud, did not even notice our arrival. The bill of debt is for 117 zlotys. This represents taxes covering four years. The clerk asks the women to empty the drawers of the furniture. The women have offered forty zlotys, which are laid down on the table. They empty the drawers, moaning as they do so. The two caftans want nothing to do with the scene. They stare at their hands as they wave them in front of their eyes. The women weep. The three young boys sway, totally engrossed in their Hebrew. The women remove the extensions of the tables. The caftans still do not see anything, and the kids grow more and more excited over the holy book. The clerk orders the women to open the cupboards. The women fall on their knees. And since they are sobbing loudly, the three young boys raise their voices.

The cart driver, who has found some helpers, takes away the sideboard first. The women utter terrifying cries. The two caftans do not make a move. The three boys read ever more loudly. Then they take away the cupboard, the table, an armchair. The ritual candelabrum, which cannot legally be seized, is moved aside and the piece of furniture it stood on is taken away.

Now the room is empty.

Then, one of the two caftans gets up; he sees that the clerk was serious. With a noble gesture, he draws from his pocket two one-hundred-zloty bills and says, "Here you are!"

The furniture is brought back.

The women cried in vain.

The three boys continued to study.

The father picks up the seven-branched candelabrum and piously replaces it on the piece of furniture that has just been returned!

CHAPTER 18

The Miracle-Making Rabbi

On Friday morning in Warsaw, buses are waiting at the far end of the city, at a place called Lublin Union.

Pigs on the way to the cattle market would not find these buses comfortable.

These are the buses of Gora-Kalwaria.*

Twenty meters from this stop, a little station houses a little train. On its route, the little train also stops at Gora-Kalwaria. On this day, the square and the station are bustling with Jews dressed in caftans and flat caps. Parcels clasped in their hands, busy looks on their faces, filling the air with their Yiddish, they storm carriages and buses.

They are going to "make Shabbat" with the illustrious miracle-making rabbi of Gora-Kalwaria.

Gora-Kalwaria, "Mount Calvary," is a village situated thirty kilometers from Warsaw. It has only two thousand inhabitants, but it is one of the nerve centers of eastern European Jewry. It is here that the celebrated *tzaddik* Alter, successor to the Baal Shem Tov who carried the *Zohar* across the Carpathians, tries to make contact with God

---

* The Yiddish name for Gora-Kalwaria is Gur, home of the renowned Gerer Hassidic dynasty.

just as radio fans try every evening to find the right wavelength. The Baal Shem Tov, as mentioned before, was the first miracle-making rabbi. And Rebbe Alter, the *tzaddik* of Gora-Kalwaria, my friend, is another!

My friend? It is to be believed, since he did not hesitate to interrupt a celestial conversation – albeit not for long – in order to conduct one with me. Is there more than one *goy** per year who can boast of such an honor? Addressing kings, eminent personalities, colleagues is nothing, but a saint?

Now, talking to Catholic saints is no problem. They're all dead! All you need to do is enter a church and talk to a statue. Any man who has lost a cent can pray to Saint Anthony of Padua.† But Jewish saints are alive. And getting to shake their hands is a long, drawn-out affair!

The Jewish elite of Warsaw labored eight days on my behalf. The chief rabbi, eminent lawyers and doctors all telephoned Mount Calvary. On the sixth day, relatives of the saint had still not been able to reach him. His body was well and truly in Gora-Kalwaria, but his spirit was elsewhere. It was wandering among clouds that were visible to our eyes but concealed Elijah the prophet, who had descended over the home of Rebbe Alter expressly so that the spirit of the Rebbe could rise and converse with him.

"Send a telegram," I said to my lawyer. "It's now or never!"

On the seventh day, the spirit of Rebbe Alter reinhabited his body. Elijah must have been in an excellent mood, or so I presume, for the *tzaddik* answered, "The foreigner may come."

On the eighth day…

I arrived in Gora-Kalwaria.

---

*   Yiddish term for Gentile. The original Biblical term *goy* signifies a nation.

†   Patron saint of lost articles.

Holy Abraham, I already knew this country! It was here, three years beforehand, during the Piłsudski coup, that a hundred vultures had surrounded my car, those walking vultures that Eastern Jews, as you already know, strangely resemble. But today, they no longer frighten me. In two months, one becomes accustomed to the shadows of the beards and the lengths of the caftans. Here is the only street, the little square, with the same wig-wearing women behind their stalls.

"Have you been here before? Those two over there say they have seen you before," says Ben.

These Jews examine passersby with such scrutiny that, three years later, they are able to point you out!

***

We are now in the country of a *tzaddik*. Israel has a dozen miracle-making rabbis. It is not a lot for six million disciples (we are not counting the Jews of western Europe or America, for whom the utterances of the leaders of the day are more persuasive than those of Elijah the prophet!). Of the twelve who hold the distinction of *wunderrabbi*, four come from important dynasties: Alexander, Radzin, Belz and Gora-Kalwaria, since the position of miracle-making rabbi is hereditary. What is a *tzaddik*? He is the terrestrial interpreter of the will of God. By isolating himself, he enters into contact with the Lord. Did not the *tzaddik* of Kotzk, known as the Great Silent One, remain silent and solitary for thirty years? The role of a *tzaddik* is to lead the people of Israel. Czars, kings, dictators can talk, but the *tzaddik* has the last word. He is also a healer. He controls nervous diseases. He drives away the *dybbuk* (tormented dead spirit) from the body of a possessed person. His great expertise is making a woman fertile. He succeeds from time to time... And each miracle-making rabbi is, of course, the enemy of other miracle-making rabbis.

Fortunate are the villages where they are born. They enjoy the benediction of the Lord, total benediction encompassing the spiritual and the material. The white bread of the Sabbath or even that of other days does not lack when there is a *tzaddik* around. Donations pour down over a miracle maker. One of the most bizarre, and to my mind novel, forms of donation is the percentage he receives from commercial and industrial transactions. Before any transaction, pious Jews make a pledge of 10 percent of their profits to the *tzaddik*. Thus, one sees magnificent debtors disembarking at Gora-Kalwaria in order to pay their miraculous debts. Fifty thousand francs in profit, five thousand francs for the *tzaddik*!

During the holy festivals of spring and autumn, the Jews of eastern Europe set out to pay their respects to their holy men. They make pilgrimages to them just as the Muslims make pilgrimages to Mecca. Ten thousand, fifteen thousand descend on Gora-Kalwaria at Passover and Yom Kippur and erect their tents. Just as, during the exodus from Egypt, they camped in the desert around Moses, today they camp in the plains of Poland around the house of their *tzaddik*. Then it is the occasion of the celebrated meal, instituted by the Baal Shem Tov.* You cannot claim to have seen anything until you see Jews fighting wildly over carp bones – the leftovers from the plate of a living saint.

Ulica Pijarska. We are certainly in the right street, since it is the only one in Gora-Kalwaria. It is Sunday. The Jews who came to make Shabbat with the *tzaddik* are leaving for the railway station. Had we come to assassinate the saint, they would not have stared at us more suspiciously.

---

*   Reference to the *tisch* – when Hassidim gather together to share a meal at the table of their Rebbe.

"Yes," Ben tells them, "we are going to see him. We too. And we are even going to touch him!"

"Tell them that I plan to pluck a hair from his beard."

"Be quiet or they will stone us."

Now we are in the home of the *tzaddik*'s brother-in-law, the great introducer of ambassadors. What a fantastic house! The impression that we have suddenly wandered into a Rembrandt painting is so great that we stop in our tracks so as not to rip the canvas. There, in a corner, an extraordinary prophet, head covered by a *tallit*, a prayer box on his forehead and leather bracelet around his left arm, is sitting on a worm-ridden throne chair, a bucket of water at his side, slowly tracing Hebrew letters on a parchment. Several quills and various inks lie in front of him. He is one of those celebrated *sofrim*, a Torah scribe. Let us stop and admire him. Each time he has to write the name of the Eternal, he raises his eyes, blesses Jehovah,* washes his hand in the bucket of water and changes his quill. Sometimes, when the task proves awesome, he leaves his throne to go and plunge his entire body in a ritual bath. Then the copyist of God dries himself, dons again his clothes, *tallit* and box and resumes work.

The *tzaddik*'s brother-in-law is terribly affable. He shows us a thousand-year-old copy of the Talmud. For having been handled so much, its pages are worn like the steps of an ancient staircase. He also tells us that the miracle-making rabbi is not a recluse... He just stood for the third time under the bridal canopy, and his new wife is joyful as a bird and no less delectable than hot wine from Zion. Jerusalem has seen him twice and every year he takes the waters at Marienbad. He has correspondents the world over, even in

---

*   Londres is not entirely correct. Before writing the name of God, a Torah scribe utters the words "*l'shem kedushat hashem*" (for the sanctity of the name).

America, and, since I come from Paris, do I know rue Lamartine? Well, the Paris correspondent of the miracle-making rabbi lives at no. 28 rue Lamartine. I greeted this news with a tinge of jubilation. Henceforth, when I meet a Jewish friend on rue Lamartine, I'll envisage him pledging 10 percent of his profits to the wizard of Gora-Kalwaria!

But for the moment, let us cross Pijarska Street. The saint's house is on the opposite side.

It is a farm inside a courtyard. In this courtyard five Jews stand motionless like cypress trees. We climb three steps and cross an antechamber crammed with thirty Jews, eyes ablaze, perhaps thirty debtors! The brother-in-law pushes a door. We find ourselves in the saint's school, his private *yeshiva*. Adolescents and old men bend over the same Talmud or the same *Zohar*, and the same fervor inhabits those close to their birth and those close to their death. The heads here are the most sensational I have seen, as yet, during this voyage. This one looks like a merino sheep and that bald one resembles an old condor. You would think that the one is about to bleat and the other about to bat his wings. The brother-in-law pushes another door. At the far end of a large, empty room, a rather short, stocky, well-fed man wearing a luxurious fur hat, hands tucked behind his back like Napoleon, is standing near a window that gives onto a dung heap. He grimaces as he looks at us.

It is the *tzaddik*.

His beard is white and his gaze as hard as a diamond. It is a gaze that impels the visitor to gather his wits together.

Not a chair in this throne room. Just his table and his armchair, that is all. This authority does not wish to be indebted to anything external.

Now we face him. He questions his brother-in-law and extends his hand to me. As for Ben, he is granted no more than a disdainful raise of the little finger. If I am a dog, Ben belongs to an even lower species: a Jew who has shaved his beard is not far removed from a pig. Once the polite exchanges have been translated, I say to Ben, "He is giving you the evil eye, old chap!"

The *tzaddik* does not answer Ben's questions.

Ben is vexed. He tells me that he has never set eyes before on such a Buddha! He is going to speak to him in Hebrew, to show him that he knows as much as the *tzaddik*.

"Since he has been to Palestine, let him tell you what he thinks about Zionism."

Ben asks the question.

The sound of Hebrew tickles the saint's ear. He answers. Ben grimaces.

"What did he say?"

"He says that Hebrew is the language of prayer and not of visits! I am going to ask him in what language he converses with the prophet Elijah!"

"No. Tell him instead that I witnessed horrific poverty among his Jews and I want to hear what he has to say about that."

"He says that one must rely only on God."

"And on money?"

"Only on Jewish money."

"And on Palestine?"

Ben is happy to return to the subject. It is clear that it embarrasses the *tzaddik*, who turns his head away.

"Go ahead, Ben!"

Accustomed to conversing with the prophet Elijah, Rebbe Alter is not someone whom a miserable little Jew from the Marmarosh Mountains can disconcert for long. He turns around, glares at my dear redhead with eagle eyes and says something.

"He says that men are not going to teach the Eternal a lesson."

Turning toward me, the rabbi gave me a sort of smile and favored me with a few words in Yiddish.

"He says he was pleased to meet us."

In short, the saint had had enough of us!

Not knowing where to find a candle, which I would have lit as I left, I searched for the collection box in which I could drop a few alms at least. But I could not find one, so I left.

"Extend to him at least a finger," I told Ben, who was making a fast exit like an ill-mannered lout.

"Let him ascend to heaven – it won't be my hand that holds him back!"

So we left the house of miracles, followed by a gaze of steel.

CHAPTER 19

Goodbye, Ben!

W e are about to part, dear Ben. Of course, we are not going to cry; but we have become good friends since that evening in Mukachevo when you tried to prove to me that parrots nest in the Carpathian Mountains. And what cold we experienced together! Where can our Wandering Jew from the Marmarosh Mountains be at this moment? Did he arrive? And in which country? Did he manage to sell his candles? And that landing at five in the morning in Oradea-Mare, with your pack on your back. We never replaced that *mezuzah*, which was not nice of us. Do your relatives in the Galanterie still shudder at the memory of the pogroms? Perhaps I will see the pioneer from Kishinev again in Jerusalem? Did you know that, in his anti-Zionist fury, the watchmaker from Cernauti sabotaged my watch? Those poor Jews of Lwow! And those of Cracow – what a pity they refused to let themselves be photographed. I missed out on the most beautiful heads. And Nalewki? If the miracle-making rabbi had been less intolerant toward you, our meeting would have gone well. And now you are returning to your Subcarpathian Russia…

We walked around Warsaw, Ben and I.

"When you get to Palestine," he said, "observe everything closely and write and tell me whether the enterprise is worth the effort."

"You are a man of little faith!"

"I am a Jew who seeks his destiny."

"You found it in Czechoslovakia."

"When one of your alpinists finds shelter during a climb, does he believe he has reached the summit of Mont Blanc? For us Jews from this part of Europe, Mont Blanc is still in the clouds. I took refuge in the Marmarosh Mountains. Others remained in Russia, Poland or Romania. But do not be deceived by our temporarily sedentary state. None of us believe that we have arrived. We are all still walking toward an inaccessible peak."

"You, perhaps."

"All of us! Time has not calmed the souls of any one of us."

"I recall, however, that in Whitechapel I heard some families say they regretted having left Russia. 'Oh, if only we could have remained in Russia,' they said."

"It was an admission, not a regret. To regret does not mean to be attached. We often regret a situation that was far from satisfactory. The Jews of Russia? They know they are enjoying a truce now. Bolshevism has brought them peace. But every regime that follows Bolshevism will bring them war. And they will pay the price. It will be even worse than Petliura's pogroms. Everyone knows this and it will be ghastly. In Poland? The situation is worse than it's ever been. In Romania, the antagonism is blatant. In Czechoslovakia, there is neutrality but also neglect. That's the picture. Who wouldn't want to get out?"

"The Jewish people, my dear Ben."

"The Jewish people are like all other peoples. There are some who are content and some who are discontent. And those who are content take no interest in those who are discontent. What distinguishes the Jewish people is that it has been torn apart. Every nation has its own image. All you have to do is look at the images on coins. They are imprinted with the image of a rooster, a woman's head, a sheaf, an eagle or a king. The image of the Jewish people should be Cubist: arms on one side, head on the other, legs in a corner and trunk missing! The Jews of America and Western Europe represent the head. The seven million living in Russia, Poland and Romania represent the trunk. Those who, like me, are walking toward the unknown, represent the legs."

"And the arms?"

"They are all the wretched folk who extended their arms to you. As for the head, it found another body. It's the most marvelous successful surgical operation I ever heard of. The head left us one day, carried off by two eagles and, after multiplying during its voyage, settled on the shoulders of England, France, Germany and America. Since then, nurtured on foreign blood, it has completely forgotten us. When cruel convulsions attack the trunk, it does not even hear the latter's moans. We are well and truly split into four: the Jews of your part of the world – the assimilated ones; the Jews here – the imprisoned ones; the Jews of Palestine – the enlightened ones; and Jews like me."

"The alpinists?"

"An alpinist who, till now, has only managed to climb the Carpathian Mountains!

"Do you remember that school in St. George Street* and the students with sidelocks and round hats? Well, I used to be one of those students. Look at me: my forehead is the proof. In Nalewki, I went begging to pay for my studies. At night, I guarded the store of an old-clothes vendor in an alley off Goose Street. I imbibed the

---

*   Ulica Sto-Jerska in Nalewki (the Warsaw ghetto).

Talmud fourteen hours a day straight from the bottle and, ten years ago, you would have seen me, intoxicated like the others, swaying on a bench in the Mesivta. I was on the way to becoming an imprisoned Jew, imprisoned by his religion and by Poland, but they did not find me a wife, so I came to my senses just as I was about to become a rabbi.

"I won't forget my arrival at the Podolsk community: a mud-steeped village, two famished dogs searching, trembling, for food. A Polish peasant was cleaning a windowpane from the inside. A Jew was pushing a cart full of sheepskins. I saw wooden houses with thatched roofs. This was where six years of crazy studies had led me. My body shuddered in its caftan. A rabbi? A teacher of Israel? But where? Here? For thirty, forty years until my death. I felt so *nebbish*, so unfortunate a man, that as I walked toward my future sheep's pen I kept repeating, 'No! No! No!'

"The first night in my *chata* [hut] decided my fate. In a dream, I saw the world. Since I did not have a homeland, could I not choose one? The great beacons of hope danced before my eyes: London, Paris, New York, Berlin! Should I too abandon my caftan, cut my sidelocks and assimilate? My memory skills had been so well honed in the Mesivta that I would be able to learn everything in one day – French, English and Spanish, the customs of these nations and how to wear a jacket. I was in turmoil and the religious spirit began to leave me.

"I spent a week in Podolsk. Then, drawn by the unknown and without telling anyone, I took the train back to Warsaw. What can I say? I went to the market at the far end of Zoliborska, where people pull clothes out of the disinfectant oven to put on their backs. I acquired my first jacket; it was green. And my first hat was grey. But my trousers being yellowish, I hardly looked like an elegant European. Cutting off one's sidelocks is sacrilegious. And yet! A mirror in Nalewki told me that I could no longer go around with a Jewish head on a Polish suit. The two great curls of hair that fell from my temples belied the hat and jacket, my first act of assimilation! It was a trader in Pauska Street who cut them off. And since Pauska means *gentlemen*, he pointed out that I could not have chosen a better street to make my formal entry into the world.

"So I found myself facing life.

"Did my conscience protest at the fact that I no longer observed the Jewish laws? Indeed, if I listened closely, I thought I could hear it speaking harshly to me. 'My son,' I told myself, 'do not hearken to it. Until now, you led a privileged life, you learned to live in a world that does not exist. You know how to behave toward Moses, but what is the connection between the world of today and Moses?'

"So I worked as a private tutor for Hungarian Jews and went on holiday with them to Italy. With the money I saved, I spent six months in Grenoble, where I learned French. Spanish holiday makers in Uriage then took me to Barcelona. I went to Vienna. From Vienna to Prague. You met me in the Marmarosh Mountains. I've sniffed around everywhere a little but I haven't yet found my bone. My brother in New York has not been in contact. I missed a departure for Brazil. I am thirty years old and I am still sleeping under the bridges of other nations!"

"We'll try to find you a bed, Ben."

"Happy are your Jews who feel at home! All of us, here, are not at home. That is why we have to watch our movements, behave as though we are always on a visit, and act more politely than anyone else. We are accused of being obsequious. But we are no more than guests wherever we live. When you are at home, in your own home, you do as you like. You are free to lunch in shirtsleeves. A guest, even lowly guests like ourselves, must be more correct. Did you know that Jews like me are the most unfortunate? Religious Jews wait for the Messiah. Assimilated Jews become lords in England or deputies in France. The Zionists are living out their dream. But we, the deserters of the ghetto? We are the real wandering Jews.

"This is why nothing angers me more than compatriots who live in luxury. Do they think they will continue to live for centuries in countries where they happen to reside just by chance? A people such as ours must have its walking stick always at hand, for the laws of its host countries can become so harsh that it is regularly forced to move elsewhere. This people must therefore not squander its money, but save it in order to flee. Money is the passport of the Jews."

I looked at my companion, my subtle redhead who, for the last two months, had plucked his brains for me, like a musician his violin.

"In short, Ben, what do you want?"

"If Zionism has a future, make sure you write and tell me this from Jerusalem. I will go there. And I shall live there as a Jew. If not, think of me when you return to Paris. I speak thirteen languages. Do you think there is a place for me in a shipping company, for example? I could also become English, but since you are French and you offered your services…"

We were walking on Marszalskowska, in the direction of Bacchus, a famous Warsaw restaurant. Ben bought a Yiddish newspaper and perused it.

"What year do you believe this is?" he asked.

"1929."

"No, it is 5690." He pointed to the date at the top the paper.

"For readers of this paper, the world began with Adam. That is correct, but I want you to remember this point which is, perhaps, the light in all this darkness. In the Marmarosh Mountains, Bessarabia, Bukovina, Galicia, Nalewki, yesterday in Gora-Kalwaria, we were in the year 5690. In fifteen days' time, when you land in Palestine, you will find yourself in the tenth year of Zionism.* Do not lose sight of these two poles."

One leg on Adam, the other on Lord Balfour – what a balancing act! I immediately felt the need to regain my equilibrium. We duly arrived at the entrance to Bacchus. The two men who had lost count of the year pushed the door open. Perhaps they would find 1929 again at the bottom of a bottle – or, if need be – a barrel!

---

*   This is an approximation; the Balfour Declaration was issued on November 2, 1917.

CHAPTER 20

The Promised Land

Here is the sun! I left Warsaw in the year 5690. Now I enter year 10.

Fifteen days are behind us. I made a voyage and crossed the Mediterranean. The *Sphinx*, not that of Egypt but of the Messageries Maritimes shipping company, lies facing Jaffa. I am on the *Sphinx*. In front of us lies Palestine.

> For thy waste and thy desolate places and the land of thy destruction shall even now be too narrow by reason of the inhabitants.

Thus said Isaiah (49:19) in year 20 of the reign of Ozias, in year 3219 of the world.*

> His Majesty's Government view with favour the establishment in Palestine of a national home for the Jewish people, and will use their best endeavours to facilitate the achievement of this object.

---

* Ozias refers to King Uzziah. The prophet Isaiah is believed to have lived under four kings: Uzziah, Yotam, Ahaz and Hezekiah. In the Jewish calendar, the year 3219 corresponds roughly to the twentieth year of the reign of King Hezekiah.

Thus said Lord Balfour in year 7 of the reign of King George V, in year 1917 of Jesus Christ.

> His Majesty's Government regard the realization of Dr. Weizmann's dream that Palestine should become as Jewish as England is English as impracticable and have no such aim in view. Nor have they at any time contemplated, as appears to be feared by the Arab delegation, the disappearance or the subordination of the Arabic population, language, or culture in Palestine.*

Thus said Winston Churchill in year 12 of the reign of King George V, in year 1922 of Jesus Christ.[†]

> Herzl! Herzl! Your dream has come true!

Thus spoke Isaac Cohen, a passenger of the *Sphinx*, when he set eyes on the Holy Land, year 4 of the presidency of Gaston Doumergue, year 1929 of Jesus Christ.

No one has spoken since.

---

*   Londres alters the text of the British White Paper slightly. This translation represents Londres's French representation. The actual document does not mention Chaim Weizmann but reads as follows: "Unauthorized statements have been made to the effect that the purpose in view is to create a wholly Jewish Palestine. Phrases have been used such as that Palestine is to become 'as Jewish as England is English.' His Majesty's Government regard any such expectation as impracticable and have no such aim in view. Nor have they at any time contemplated, as appears to be feared by the Arab delegation, the disappearance or the subordination of the Arabic population, language, or culture in Palestine."

†   The quotation is from the British White Paper of 1922.

***

Those Arab boatmen are going to drop my suitcases in the sea. Not so fast! Don't be so clumsy! Ah, the pirates! Here are the twin cities of this coastline: the old one, Muslim Jaffa; the new one, Jewish Tel Aviv. Jaffa with its minarets, Tel Aviv with its synagogue dome. The new has won over the old. The Jews have worked hard. Ten years ago there was only a sand dune on this spot. Tel Aviv is so big already! The city has sprouted like Casablanca. It is a milestone in history! For nineteen centuries, a people has waited for this city! The Jews now have a capital. It is here. I can see it – Israel has been resuscitated!

Thirty-four Jewish men and seventeen Jewish women from Poland have just emerged from the depths of the *Sphinx*. They stand on deck, like an animated illustration of the word of the Lord: "Thy sons and thy daughters will come from afar."* For the last eight days, they have been doing a little cooking and reciting a lot of prayers down in the hold. And here they are, this morning, shouting with joy and waving their arms like madmen and madwomen. They, who until today would have respectfully prolonged their journey in order to spare you contact with their shadow, are stepping on your toes. They strike their hearts and touch their temples and shoulders. Yes! It is truly you! Do not doubt it. Next year in Jerusalem – that's today!

Into the boats! Into the boats! The Poles rush down the gangway as though they were scaling the ladder of the beatitudes! And, like horizontal palms, the oars carry us off joyfully toward the Promised Land.

The gateway that the land opens before us is not very big. Jaffa does not have a port. This little strait between two rocks, where

---

*   Loose translation of Isaiah 60:4.

a stormy sea froths, constitutes the passageway. I understand why the Jews waited a long time before returning: the entry is hardly appealing. The Poles have stopped gesticulating. They are huddled in the back of the first boat. Their backs have, suddenly, resumed their hereditary stoop. A man wearing a fez jumps on the helm; the rowers shout in order to frighten fear away. Get off! Get off! Will we pass through? Of course! We always pass through!

The danger over, the Jews straighten their backs. They stand up in the boat and begin to sing. They wish that the land would come to them in the same way that they are going toward it, in order to kiss it all the more quickly. On shore, the Muslims are watching us. Their gaze is far from welcoming! Did you flee from the pogroms of Europe in order to fall into those of the Orient? *Shalom* may mean "peace be with you," but wherever you Jews utter this greeting, you are met with war!

We disembark. We are on holy ground. The Jews fall on their knees and kiss it. But we do not waste our time:

Arabadji![*] Head straight to Tel Aviv!

The Arab carriage driver takes off. Dust surrounds my carriage and seems to carry it like the clouds carried that of the Lord. So the Orient has not lost its habit of frying candles in a frying pan? Let's not talk about the smell! Trundling along, we leave Jaffa. The road becomes wider and the ground gives way to asphalt, the dust settles. I am already on the Tel Aviv road.

From Whitechapel, Prague, the Marmarosh Mountains, Transylvania, Kishinev, Cernauti, Lwow, Cracow, Vilna, Lodz, Warsaw, Jewish family names left their store signs and preceded me. Goldman, Appelbaum, Lipovich, Blum, Diamond, Rapoport, Levy, Mendel, Elster, Goldberg, Abram, Berliner, Landau, Isaac, Toby,

---

[*]   Coach driver, in Arabic.

Rosen, Davidovich, Smith, Brown, Lewinstein, Solomon, Jacob, Israel, hello again! I have crossed the sea, but found the same family!

Herzl, the prophet of the boulevards, as Jerome and Jean Tharaud irreverently called him, had dreamed of the first Jewish city rising gently on the shores of the Mediterranean, catching the eye like a spring hill.

Tel Aviv! The Spring Hill, here it is!

For his part, Isaiah had predicted of the city:

> I will lay thy foundations with sapphires. And I will make thy windows of agates and thy gates of carbuncles and all thy borders of pleasant stones.[*]

Clearly, Isaiah was a pure soul who did not know much about building contractors! One can make wise prophecies but have no idea how to draw up an estimate.

Herzl was much closer to reality. The agates, sadly, are nothing but reinforced cement!

***

Tel Aviv! The only city in the world with a population entirely of Jews.

I left the *arabadji*. One must go on foot to enjoy such wonders. A revolution passed before my eyes. Where are my caftans, my beards, my sidelocks? Here are my Jews: heads uncovered, clean-shaven, with open collars, firm steps and chests raised high in the air. They no longer hug the walls, honestly! They walk with a military step, in the middle of the pavement, without worrying about having to cede their place to a Pole, a Russian or a Romanian. It's a miracle!

---

[*]   Isaiah 54:11–12.

Their backbones have straightened. Every back has thrown off the invisible burden of its race. I no longer have any effect on them. No eyes examine me furtively. Now, it is I who stops and questions. They keep going, with cold, proud gazes. From time to time an extraordinary creature appears: a caftan, a beard, curls! As they pass him, the others discreetly shrug their shoulders. Who is this ghost?

And Jewish women? They have thrown their wigs into the garbage, cut their hair and exposed their breasts to the air!

It's a metamorphosis.

Herzl Street! Edmond de Rothschild Boulevard! Max Nordau Street! The synagogue, the main monument in the process of being completed, seems to say it all. It is like a flag floating over a camp. The sole, unrivaled flag. No crosses in its shadow, no minarets in its radius. Just as when the Temple dominated Jerusalem, before the Church of the Holy Sepulcher and the Mosque of Omar.

At first you think that Tel Aviv, so young, can barely have more than a handful of houses, a little city that one can take in at a glance. But you will be surprised. Where you expected to find the end of the world, you find a boulevard. Rows of houses are followed by rows of houses. A camp perhaps, but not a flying camp.* There are trees here!

The Hill of Spring† has been laid out with flair. None of those American grids. The streets, squares, boulevards, avenues intercross whimsically. It is bright, spacious, sunny and all white. It is gay. It emanates a fierce determination to leave the ghetto behind. You almost expect to see all these Jews pitched on the pavements, mouths open, lovingly imbibing liberty.

---

*   A military camp designed to remain in constant motion.

†   Tel Aviv means "hill of spring" in Hebrew. Londres translates the name literally as "colline du Printemps."

So many dentists! One on each floor. On the doors, there are almost as many forceps as bells. This is the price you pay, wretched nation, for having suffered so much* for nearly two thousand years!

And hairdressers? Any man who still has hair on his face in Tel Aviv is an obstinate goat. Every three or four houses, a hairdresser beckons to you. It is a revolt against the Bible. "Do not shave your beards,"† said the Lord. Down with the Lord! Enter, Jews of Galicia, of Volhynia, of Lithuania, of Bessarabia, citizens of Berdichev and other "chevs"! I shave, my wife shaves, my children shave, my mother-in-law shaves. The day being too short to shave everyone, we also shave at night. Even at three in the morning, don't hesitate, press the emergency bell! You haven't shaved since Moses. How will you make up for lost time?

And lawyers? Oh, God! You have hardly gathered together in the Holy Land, and you Jews are already bickering on every street corner. Because all these lawyers are eating, and if they are eating, it means that you are quarreling. You number forty thousand inhabitants in Tel Aviv, forty thousand Jews without one *goy*, and you need so many lawyers?

And you, doctors? Everyone in Tel Aviv is sprightly. The deserters of the ghetto left their pale countenances behind in the Carpathians. There is not one sick person in the street, and people sing in their homes. What are you doing in this place? Are you waiting for the next pogrom in order to have work?

A man who just left the sons of Abraham in the Carpathians or on the Vistula and who, fifteen days later, finds them again on the shores of the Oriental Mediterranean transformed into the sons

---

*   Londres uses a French idiom, "for having eaten mad cow," meaning for having suffered a life of privation.

†   Leviticus 19:27.

of Theodor Herzl has truly experienced amazement! For the time being, there is no point playing the economist, drawing up a commercial balance sheet or stroking one's forehead with a bookkeeper's fingers. Those who become pale over statistics ignore the fact that statistics themselves pale quickly. Furthermore, is it necessary to know whether the dentists, hairdressers, lawyers, doctors, traders and boot shiners are doing good business? One day a Jew had a dream. He saw his compatriots unfasten their chains, fly away, cross the sea and alight transfigured on ancestral soil. From a state of slavery, they became free men. In their hearts, pride replaced shame. Confidence replaced fear. And each one could stand at his window and shout, "I am a Jew! This is my glory!" without risking being tied on the spot to the tail of a wild mare. Open your eyes, the dream will not unravel – it is cemented in Tel Aviv!

Hebrew has been resuscitated.

Having emerged from the tomb of the Talmud,[*] the Hebrew language hugs the coastline from Gaza to Acre, flies from Mount Tabor to the Mount of Olives, from Jericho to Tiberias, and runs along the Jezreel Valley. It is in Hebrew that a child calls his mother, that a lover lies to his beloved, and that neon signs entice passersby.

Descended directly from the crown of God, the sacred letters flash today above doorways.

The city has been built.

Here is the high school, concert hall, municipality, theater, water tower, post office, sanatorium and hospital.

Here is the beach and here is the casino.

Here are the cafés, cinemas and night clubs.

Here are blocks of flats and private homes.

---

[*]   The Talmud is actually written in Aramaic. Modern Hebrew derives from the language of the Torah (Old Testament).

In 1908, no houses; in 1920, two hundred forty; in 1921, one thousand seven; in 1926, three thousand fifty; in 1929, almost five thousand!

"Thou shalt be built," says its motto.

From the moment the first stone was laid, the Arab responded, "Thou shalt be destroyed!"

CHAPTER 21

At the Price of Bloodshed

It is not dishonorable to admit that, in December 1929, we were strolling in the city of Haifa. We were there, as we could have been anywhere else, and always for the same, excellent reason that one has to be somewhere. The weather was quite good. The rainy season hardly troubled us. I was focusing my eyes on the far side of the bay: on Acre. I was thinking of Napoleon, who had a hard time there, and of the mosque built in honor of his defeat, whose dome can undoubtedly be said to be one of the most beautiful breasts on the Oriental skyline. I was living quietly and effortlessly when the Arabs descended Mount Carmel, each holding a bludgeon in his hand.

Against whom was their hostility directed?

My innocence in all things evident, it could not have been me. The British soldiers? None were around. Preceded by the flag of the Prophet, the Arabs rushed past. I followed them. They stopped at the edge of the sea, where, had they wanted to go on, they would have had to walk on water.

A boat bobbed up and down in the harbor.

It was the boat that was the target of the Arabs. They waved their cudgels threateningly at it. On the boat, people were singing passionately. These were the first Zionists who were arriving.

***

Had the Arabs never seen Jews in Palestine? They certainly had! The tragedies of history, in Czarist Russia, had driven several thousand miserable souls to this illustrious but forsaken land. The date was 1882. Saved from the pogroms, ruined by them and probably impelled by them, Bessarabians and Ukrainians, imbued with biblical literature, had adopted the name of Hovevei Zion (Lovers of Zion) and had come, as in the time of the Ark of the Covenant, to marry their nascent hopes with the ancestral soil.

The land was less bountiful than that described in their holy Torah. It did not flow with milk and honey, and only had a little water. And the only singing that was heard was the buzzing of mosquitoes. But does a lover, a young lover, fear obstacles? He leaps across the balcony until the balcony gives way under his weight. This was how it was. Destitute, crushed, sick and wan, the Hovevei Zion pioneers dragged their disillusions and their malaria to a land that Moses himself had thought would be more hospitable.

They would all have perished had an angel not passed over! He dropped over them money, quinine, milk and honey.

He spoke with the Turks the language of the checkbook. And, just as a country would have done with a new colony, he sent a representative, administrators and a health corps. He established schools and hospitals. He settled debts. He advanced loans. He told Israel: "Rise and walk." And Israel rose and walked. The angel was the baron.

In Palestine, there were prophets, judges, kings and heroes – but there is only one baron. Just as in Italy there is only one duce.

The baron of Palestine is Mr. Edmond de Rothschild. He is the only individual on earth who owns a colony. Which is altogether different from owning a racing stable!

Let us take our leave of him and return to our subject.

It was neither the Lovers of Zion nor the baron's protégés who riled the Arabs' blood. Of course, had they been told to pull the beards of these Jews, the Arabs would have reveled in the task. But such a pastime did not present itself. The Arabs tolerated the pious Jews of Jerusalem and they did not create a rumpus over the unfortunate souls from Bessarabia who sought the soothing protection of Mr. de Rothschild's golden arms.

Allah was above such things.

But then came the war. While Turkey, which governed Palestine, was on one side, the other side, via the Intelligence Service of His Majesty the king of England, tried to win the Arabs over. If victory fell to the British, they promised to establish an Arab kingdom, a great kingdom as magnificent as the legend.

Victory came. England puffed its cheeks and exhaled. The Arab kingdom vanished. Israel took its place.

There is no point laboring over historical texts. Whether the settlement of the Jews in Palestine is called a "national home" rather than a "Jewish state" does not alter the fact. And the fact is this: this time, the Jews were arriving not as beggars, but as citizens. They were no longer asking for hospitality – they were taking possession of the land. They would no longer be a tolerated people, but equal. And Abraham glowed while Muhammad covered his face.

A story will help you understand this metamorphosis. It dates from General Allenby's entry into Jerusalem. A Jew knocks on an Arab's door. The Jew and the Arab are old friends. They must even like each other a lot to rise above the synagogue-mosque divide. The Arab opens the door to the Jew.

"I curse your father," says the Jew. "I curse him five times."

An unpardonable insult in this country. The Arab is thunderstruck. He asks, "Why? What have I done?"

"My friend," answers the Jew, "you will understand. Until this morning, I was your slave. If I had uttered such a blasphemy, you would have informed the police and the police would have thrown me in prison and beaten me like a dog. Yesterday, I was a dog. But, today, I am a man. I can say to you, with no danger, what *you* could say to me with no danger. It is nineteen centuries of oppression that I have cast off with this blasphemy. I could not restrain myself. Forget it, forgive me and come let me embrace you..."

The heads of the Young Jews swam with the intoxicating wine of independence. A heroic period began. It was the start of "the bright prospect of honor, freedom and happiness" predicted by Herzl.[*]

And then something wonderful took place. Idealism overrode self-interest. The Jews, those Young Jews of Palestine, of all the nations, brought honor to humanity.

They arrived with fire in their souls. Ten thousand, twenty thousand, fifty, a hundred thousand. They were the last example of the great intellectual movements of history. Faith carried them, not toward the divine but toward the terrestrial. They came to win the right to be who they were. It was a moving sight. Doctors, teachers, lawyers, painters, poets all set out to tame the wild land with pickaxes and shovels. While one should acknowledge that the Arabs inhabited this land for centuries, it should also be noted that they did not complete the work. They lived here in the way beautiful wild creatures inhabit the jungle.

In normal life, ambition progresses from manual to intellectual labor. By giving his son a liberal education, the worker strives to push his progeny up the social ladder. The new Jews turned this tradition on its head. The doctor of law became a digger, the student a peasant. This stone breaker used to sell paintings in Moscow. This

---

[*]   Quote from Herzl's book *The Jewish State*, published in 1896.

cow herder was a violinist in Prague. This Tel Aviv hairdresser was a brilliant litigant in Lwow. This farm girl sang at the Grand Theater of Warsaw and this Jew, a former teacher of religion in Vilna, is now a shepherd on the slopes of Nazareth! A Jewish shepherd? Until now, I had only ever met Jewish bankers!

You have to be a stubborn realist to stick to an ideal! And these were truly realists, toiling, sweating…dying. The white skins went on a crusade against the mosquito, the intellectuals drained swamps, that librarian cleared rocks, and that veteran city dweller camped out in the Judean desert. Where there was once a dune, a city sprang up. Orange groves grew on red soil. Thistles gave way to wheat. The Palestine mummy was slowly coming to life.

Settlements, the name they gave to their villages, followed settlements. The country became covered with them. The names they were given exuded hope: *Tel Or*, hill of light; *Degania*, wheat of God; *Nahalat Yaakov*, heritage of Jacob; *Mishmar Hayarden*, the Jordan River guard; *Tel Hai*, hill of life; *Menorah*,* it will bring light! Little girls were no longer named Esther but Carmela (from Mount Carmel), Hermona (Mount Hermon), Yardena (Jordan River), Sharona (the Sharon plain), and Herzliya (Theodor Herzl).

The twenty-century-old exiles who spoke eighteen languages – Russian, Ruthenian, Polish, Romanian, Czech, Bulgarian, Hungarian, German, Dutch, Spanish, English, Italian, Turkish, Yemenite, Arabic, Persian, Yiddish out of a slave mentality and French out of refinement – rescued Hebrew from the abyss of time and installed it in their textbooks and on their storefronts. But you know all this!

---

*   The Menorah was the seven-branched candelabrum that stood in the Temple in Jerusalem.

Not all the combatants were heroic. There were softhearted ones, spineless ones, men of little faith and weak-legged ones unable to withstand the long marches. There were women who could not endure being parted from their dress stores, five o'clock teas and municipal street lamps. There was an exodus in the opposite direction. The Promised Land did not pay.

The signs of crisis were evident in Tel Aviv.

The English were delighted. You surely did not imagine that, by bringing Jews to Palestine, the English wanted to please the Jews. The Jews were simply pawns who could help them win the game. And once the game was won, the pawns were put back in the box. England jumped on the crisis and did its best to aggravate things. It allowed those it had brought in to leave and closed the door to those who wished to enter.

It was a period when the non-idealists thought everything was lost. People forgot the essence of the enterprise. They spoke about Zionism in terms of a strange, failed experiment. Its children's villages and communist settlements were the butt of newspaper headlines. That was exactly the issue! Zionism was never an experiment, but an idea.

And the idea was this: If there is but one Jew who has had enough of being French, English or Austrian – a Jew who wishes to live freely as a Jew – would he cling to the one piece of land where he can call himself a Jew?

Yes, he would cling to it.

Against the wishes of England, against the indifference of mediocre Jews, with money coming in from New York and other places, the new Jews were buying up Palestine, bit by bit. And they were building factories; erecting windmills; planting wheat, vineyards, barley, corn, tobacco, orange trees, banana trees, lemon trees; and, thanks to audacious projects, transforming the Jordan into a source of light.

The crisis passed.

The anxiety of the Arabs rose.

Minor massacres of Jews no longer intimidated the Jews. If the Arabs killed one Jew, the Jews killed two Arabs. Two Jews? Four Arabs! And what, you might ask, did the British do between the two sides? The British? They disappeared. None were to be seen. It was an issue of pride for them. Whereas France required an army to hold on to Syria, the British considered Palestine theirs with just six horses.

Palestine? Seven hundred thousand Arabs on one side, one hundred fifty thousand Jews on the other; the Arabs having already "filled their tank," the Jews dreamed of filling theirs.

"We shall number three hundred thousand, five hundred thousand," cried the Jew Jabotinsky, leader of the extremists, from the top of Jaffa Gate.

"We shall not let you disembark," answered the Arab Nashashibi (Ragheb Bey al-Nashashibi, mayor of Jerusalem).*

"We shall reign," Jabotinsky told me.

"They will not reign," Nashashibi responded. "We shall cede the country to them only at the price for which we bought it."

"At what price, Ragheb Bey?"

"At the price of blood, my friend."

---

* Ragheb Bey al-Nashashibi, mayor of Jerusalem 1920–1934.

CHAPTER 22

The Wailing Wall

I was walking in Jerusalem, inside the walls. It was on a late Friday afternoon. Bedecked in rabbit-skin hats and impressive silk or velvet robes whose colors were not faded enough to make one forget that they had once been lilac, sea green, canary yellow, amaranthine, dapple grey or after-the-storm sky blue, the Jews, Moses' old Jews, made their way like withered magi through the arched alleyways of the holy labyrinth. Some pulled a child by the hand, others, in groups or alone, marched with dignity as though touched by a royal finger; all were on their way to the Wailing Wall.

This section of the ancient Temple walls is all that remains of the splendor of a nation. Fifty paces long and thirty feet high, tucked within the city, this sliver of history unleashes passionate feelings in the hearts of Israel. As soon as Jews set eyes on it, they shower it with kisses. Let us follow them. Here they come. They accelerate their steps. The moment they reach the sacred site, they touch it with their lips and caress it with their hands. The older Jews have brought little stools on which they sit, eyes awash with ecstasy. On the right, three-quarters of its length is reserved for men. On the left, the last quarter is for women.* A long, discordant, poignant lament, made up of the laments of each individual, envelops the old wall like a sonorous halo.

Let's see! Is that woman over there really crying? Are those really tears that are falling, drop after drop, on that stone? Yes, they are tears. She is pretty and she is crying! She is crying outside, in front of strangers, not because of unrequited love, but because of the destruction of her people!

Noses buried in the Torah, the men sway back and forth. They pour out their heartrending prayers into the Judean wind. You'd have to be pretty unhappy to emit such moans! When they no longer sway, they pedal on the spot; those moving on only one foot resemble knife sharpeners. You can hear kisses smacking against the stones. At other times, they kiss the wall as tenderly as one kisses a dead person. Look at those two Jews; they have closed their eyes with such intensity, their faces appear to have shriveled up completely. They stand on tiptoe and proceed to sway without losing their balance. And that fellow? Arms contorted, he implores the wall as though imploring a man on whom the life of his son depends. And that one over there? He has placed his head in his right hand and is grieving so deeply that I feel the need to approach him and ask: "What's wrong, my fellow? Can I help you?" Dressed in a tobacco-colored robe, the tall, skinny fellow points a menacing fist at the sky while his neighbor, head thrown back, scrunches his face in such a way, you would think he was gargling with Cayenne pepper. Others tap the stones with thin, trembling fingers. "Israel! Israel!" exclaims the old man suddenly, as he pinches his nose vehemently,

---

* Londres may have been viewing the Western Wall from above since, traditionally, men stand on the left and women on the right.

perhaps to clear a hiccup. Exhausted, they all rest their heavy fore-heads on the comforting stones.

Night was beginning to fall.

The Jews…

CHAPTER 23

Hey! Europe!

After returning to France, I was working on my story when, early one pleasant evening, a friend pushed open my door and blurted, "They are killing *your* Jews in Jerusalem!"

I leaped from my inkpot.

The friend handed me a newspaper. They were being killed. They were being killed even several months ahead of the due date.

So I bid adieu to my pen stand and took my hat, a train and then a boat.

I set off once again for the Holy Land.

How could it be that England was deaf? A child, even a small child, had he wanted to, could have gauged the feverish state that had engulfed the land of Canaan of late. Was it not just last April in Jerusalem on the eve of the Muslim festival of Nebi Moussa (the prophet Moses; the Arabs having adopted Moses) when, after dinner, ensconced on a sofa between Ragheb Bey al-Nashashibi, the Arab mayor of the holy city and leader of the nationalist movement, and the English governor of the same holy city, the three of us had pondered the chances of calm and, particularly, the chances of trouble? Ragheb Bey is not someone who conceals his opinions. At the first opportunity, he is ready to drive the Jews away. And Ragheb

Bey said this straight to the face of the very honorable representative of His British Majesty. And His Majesty had no more one hundred forty soldiers in Palestine?

But this is not a time for theorizing. Let us get straight to the facts and, first, to Jaffa.

A small storm. A maritime breeze. The heat has returned. Eight days have passed and here we are.

We disembark.

I finish with customs. The ground is scorching hot. I call for an *arabadji*. A carriage driver runs toward me.

"The Palatin Hotel, Tel Aviv!" I tell him.

Shaking his head, the *arabadji* refuses and moves off.

Arab carriage drivers no longer travel to the Jewish city. And Jewish carriage drivers no longer come to the Arab city. So? Am I going to be stuck here in the dust, contemplating the old pigskin of my suitcase, my cherished companion?

It occurs to me that the office of Messageries Maritimes may be able to resolve the problem. I head toward it. If I were to say that the streets smell of riot, it would be fiction. They smell simply of mutton fat. I walk on, sponging off the sweat when, suddenly, in the space of a long second, Jaffa changes mood. People begin to run into their homes or into those of others. Iron grates come down. Wooden shutters slam shut. Carriages empty out of the station and hurry off to the sounds of horsewhips. The city has become engulfed in Oriental panic. What is going on?

I reach the Messageries' office.

"What's going on?"

"We don't know."

A man enters and says, "An Arab was shouting '*halas!*' as he ran."

"What does *halas* mean?"

"It means, 'it's done, it's finished!'"

"What is?"

"We don't know."

Palestine, today, is a sensitive place. No one knew because *nothing had been done, and nothing was finished.* Reason returned an hour later.

What had this land experienced, since I had left, that it had become so tense?

This is what had happened: Since July 27, the atmosphere had been heating up in Jerusalem around the Wall of Tears.[*] Having succeeded in making the Palestinian government[†] renege on its decision to maintain the status quo, the Muslims increased the height of a wall on the left side, which was deemed in poor condition, and drilled an opening at the end of the alley.

This opening answers a pressing need: to harass the Jews. The Arabs begin. At the hour of prayer, they filter in. Since the Arabs usually walk with their donkeys, the donkeys follow and, since donkeys are intelligent creatures, they make a point of wailing as they pass by the Wailing Wall. Outcry in the Jewish press. At the very same time, the Jews are holding a congress in Zurich. Telegrams to Zurich. The congress sends two of its members to London to lodge a complaint.

August 15 is a day of mourning for the Jews.[‡] It marks the destruction of the Temple. On the eve, the Jews marched in a procession to the wall. On the fifteenth, they held meetings across the country to protest the actions of the Arabs. An extraordinary event

---

[*]   Wailing Wall.

[†]   A reference to the British government then in control of Palestine.

[‡]   August 15 in 1929 fell on the ninth of Av (Tishah b'Av), the date when the Temple was destroyed. It is the major day of mourning in the Jewish calendar.

also took place on the fifteenth. Around four hundred Young Jews left Tel Aviv for Jerusalem and proudly made their way to the Wall, accompanied by a police escort. There, one of them separated from the group and made a speech. Another raised the blue-and-white flag, the new standard of the Land of Israel.

It was the least diplomatic and most ill-advised act committed by the Jews since their return to Palestine. It communicated to the Arabs that, henceforth, they would no longer be dealing with old Jews with sidelocks, but with clean-shaven, broad-shouldered, strapping fellows in open collars!

The impatience and pride of the young fellows handed the enemy the opportunity they were waiting for.

The enemy seized it.

***

The more the situation of the Jews improved in Palestine, the more the feudal privileges of the Arab chieftains came under threat. The time had come to halt the "Jewish invasion." To achieve this, the chieftains had to incite the *fellah*s (serfs), whom the Jews, in their daily lives, did not trouble too much. False rumors had already begun to do their work. As in the Middle Ages, the Jews were accused of spreading horrible diseases. Rumor had it that they were distributing poisoned sweets and fruit to Muslim children. And was it not being said that they were attacking veiled women? But the evidence was lacking. Religious fanaticism was enough to arouse the masses.

The hour had come. The guns were in place. The grand mufti, a very amiable young man, entered the picture. Hastily printed pamphlets were dispatched to the imams of villages. The imams read them out to the assembled *fellah*s. They reported that the flag, which had been raised in front of the Wall, indicated that the Jews were about to attack Muslim holy sites. And was not the Wall one of these holy sites? It was to this wall that Muhammad had attached his horse Burak before mounting him and ascending to heaven. Time was short. The Jews were going to destroy the Omar and al-Aqsa mosques. Doctored postcards depicting the Zionist flag flying over the Mosque of Omar passed from hand to hand. The religious leaders implored the Koran, "You, law of our fathers, you whom we have sworn to defend, show us our duty!"

Nothing more was needed.

On August 16, the day of Mulud, the anniversary of the birth of the Prophet, two thousand Arabs descend from the esplanade of the mosques and pour into the narrow corridor that adjoins the Wall. They shatter the beadle's old wooden table, shred and burn the books of the Psalms, tear down from the crags in the Wall all the little pieces of paper on which the Jews inscribe their naïve prayers. They beat up the old silk robes they encounter on the way.

On August 17, young Jews are playing football in the Bukharan quarter. The ball, apparently, falls on Muslim land. The *fellah*s attack the players and some are injured. One of them dies. He is buried on August 21. The Jews want the funeral procession to pass in front of Jaffa Gate, as is the custom when a dead person is honored. The police refuse. Collision. Twenty Jews wounded.

The grand mufti requests a passport from the French consulate to go enjoy the fresh air of Lebanon. Request refused.

There are still no more than one hundred forty of His Majesty's soldiers in Palestine!

***

On Friday, August 23, Saint Bartholomew's day, masses of Arabs invade Jerusalem at dawn. They march in groups, each man holding a stick or unsheathed dagger in his hand. They sing as they enter the holy city:

The religion of Muhammad
Defends its right by the sword.
We defend by the sword
The prophet Muhammad.

The big day has arrived. The pamphlets distributed by the amiable young man have not missed their target. The dagger wielders and club-armed drum majors march toward Damascus Gate. They pass in front of French religious institutes, the French hospital and Notre Dame de France:

The religion of Muhammad
Defends its right by the sword.

Today, children of Christ, do not fear: today we are after the Jews... A large, fortress-like building stands opposite Damascus Gate; it houses the offices of the British High Commissioner. Six young Jews stand outside in a group. They would do better to withdraw and leave the field to the wave of fanaticism. But they stay, all six representing the rebellion of the new Jewish soul. They have had enough of hearing that Jews only know how to hang their heads. A pride, too-long repressed, makes them forget that heroism does not always go hand-in-hand with reason. One of the six, an Austrian journalist called Dr. von Weisel, refuses to cede one inch of ground to the advancing column. A Muslim walks over Weisel. The two men stab each other. Weisel has the upper hand.

"See!" he shouts at the four English soldiers and policemen standing in front of the building, arms at rest. "A man is attacking me! I have stopped him – come and arrest him!"

The agents of authority do not move. Two Arabs approach and stab Weisel in the back.

The representatives of the law observe the scene impassively, without a hint of a frown. So why restrain oneself? The Muslims fall on the Jews, who are surprised by the events. Everyone who passes by is in for it.

The more they kill the Jews, the more the police remain immobile. As for the British high commissioner, he has gone off for a stroll in the sky, like a Zeppelin! At least, this is what it seems, since three weeks have elapsed since anyone has had news of him.

"Death to the Jews!"

"The government is with us!"

With these cries on their lips and daggers in their hands, the sons of the Prophet rampage through Jerusalem.

They attack the neighborhoods of Talpiot, Gdud Haavoda, Bet Hakerem and Bayit Vegan, Romema, Givat Shaul, Sanhedria and Mahanaim.

They kill. They sing.

Two Englishmen, Oxford students, traveling in the Holy Land, dive into the fight. Let it not be said that the English did not try to stop the macabre dance. They entreat the Muslims. They are young! They understand nothing about politics!

And the ghettos of Hebron and Safed ignite too.

Tel Joseph, Gerdi, Nahalal have to defend themselves in the Jezreel Valley.

Arab labor is decidedly cheap: the murderers receive no more than ten cigarettes for the head of each Jew.

Hey, Europe! People are bleeding in Palestine…

The "national home" has become an international slaughterhouse.

CHAPTER 24

The Soldiers of the Grand Mufti

We have to describe what happened in Hebron and in Safed. Hebron is in Judea, meaning on stony ground. Eighteen thousand Arabs, one thousand Jews. Specifically, one thousand old Jews – not necessarily elderly, but all of them ancient: Jews from another age, with sidelocks and caftans!

We are in Hebron. There is nothing more Oriental for travelers. Streets built for cinematographic dramas. OK, but all of this is Arab. Where is the ghetto? You look for it but you do not see it. Yet you were told that it is here, in the covered bazaar, between this square and this low mosque. But no ghetto! No Jews!

You ask again and you are given a guide. The guide takes you back to the covered bazaar and stops between the stall of a slipper vendor and a seller of skinned lambs.

There, in the wall, a hole; it is a door – the door to the ghetto.

You pass through the door, bent double. You straighten yourself and if until then you could see nothing, now you see something. But it is not enough to see, you must also believe. For what lies in front of you is unbelievable. This ghetto is a mountain of houses, a real mountain with peaks, passes and ravines; a wretched little mountain, belligerent, without a square centimeter of land, covered entirely by houses, entirely! In order to reach the ground floor of the second shack you have to pass across the roof of the first. From the roof of the second, you reach the entrance of the third. And so on. Where are the streets? Indeed, where are they? No streets! But I am walking, and I am not always walking on a roof! No! I climb steps, enter a corridor, lose myself in labyrinths. Thinking I have gotten to a square, I find myself in a bedroom. If a tall man were stretched out in the doorway of his house, he would have his head in his home, his feet in the neighbor's – a neighbor he eyes with ill will – one arm elsewhere and the other in the synagogue! Three interconnected synagogues crown this mad state. The sun has nothing more bizarre to warm on the entire surface of the world!

Here live one thousand Hebrews.

Not those who waved the flag at the Wailing Wall; not a thousand strapping fellows from Tel Aviv; not those hardy, determined settlers from the Jezreel Valley. One thousand Hebrews who did not come to Palestine in a ship, but in a cradle; one thousand eternal Jews. One family recently arrived from Lithuania to live a life of holiness, not of conquest, in the land of its ancestors. Tragic family!

Friends of the Arabs? Almost. In any case, certainly not enemies, since they all know each other, even by name, and have exchanged greetings for a decade, from time immemorial. Jewish Hebron was famous not for its national sentiments but for its Talmudic school.*

The Arabs did not attack Tel Aviv, but Hebron…but Safed. I am aware that Ragheb Bey al-Nashashibi, sharp as a sword, justified himself by saying, "All is fair in love and war. You don't kill who you want, but who you find. Next time, everyone is going to be grist for

---

* The Hebron Yeshiva, founded in 1924.

the mill, young and old." We make a point of telling Ragheb Bey that we will not hold him to his word. He is certainly capable of keeping it. But, today, the future is not our business.

On August 23, the day of the grand mufti, the throats of two Talmud students are slit. They were not making political speeches, their eyes were searching for Mount Sinai, in the hope of discovering the shadow of God.

The following day, beginning in the morning, the Arabs show concern for the fate of the Jews. Not all Arabs are fanatics. Purity of mind is, thankfully, not universal in the land of Islam.

"Run for your lives!" they urge the Jews.

Some offer the shelter of their roofs to the future victims. One, a friend of a rabbi, even walks all night to pitch himself in front of the house of his protégé. He guards the entrance against the madmen of his own race.

Read on.

Some fifty Jews, men and women, had taken refuge outside the ghetto, in the Anglo-Palestine Bank, which was managed by one of their own, the son of Rabbi Slonim. They were huddled in one room. The Arabs, the soldiers of the grand mufti, soon sniffed them out. It was Saturday, August 24, nine in the morning. After blowing open the door of the bank… But here's the story in a nutshell: They cut off hands, they cut off fingers, they held heads over a stove, they gouged out eyes. A rabbi stood immobile, commending the souls of his Jews to God – they scalped him. They *made off* with his brains. On Mrs. Sokolov's lap, one after the other, they sat six students from the yeshiva and, with her still alive, slit their throats. They mutilated the men. They shoved thirteen-year-old girls, mothers and grandmothers into the blood and raped them in unison.

Mrs. X—— is lying in a Jerusalem hospital. They killed her husband at her feet, then slaughtered her child in her arms. "You, you will remain alive...," the twentieth-century men told her.

Today, she was staring out the window, eyes vacant and tearless.

Rabbi Slonim, so dark, so Velasquez, is there too. He speaks: "They killed my two sons, my wife, my father-in-law, my mother-in-law."

He recounts this matter-of-factly, like a court clerk reading out an official record.

But then he cries: "In 1492, Jews who were expelled from Spain brought a Torah scroll to Hebron, a holy scroll, a divine Torah. The Arabs burned my Torah."

Rabbi Slonim wipes two tears from his burnished cheeks.

Twenty-three corpses in the room of the bank. Blood still covers the tiled floor, like a thick jelly.

> The religion of Muhammad
> Defends its right by the sword.

And you cannot imagine the grace, youth, sweetness, charm and clear complexion of the grand mufti...

***

Safed is situated in the Upper Galilee, one thousand meters in the sky. Three mountain peaks topped with houses, houses painted in whitewash – blue, pink, yellow and white. In the distance, in a hole, two hundred meters below sea level, a mirror in the shape of a lyre: the Sea of Galilee. Mirror! Lyre! Soft colors! But wait.

Like those of Hebron, the Jews of Safed are ancient Jews who cultivate...the *Zohar*! Elderly Hassidim, they sing and dance in honor of the Lord. Those who, in addition, own stores in the ghetto closed their stores six days ago. It is August 29. They did not want to excite the Arabs who, since the twenty-third, have been parading up and down, brandishing daggers and clubs and swearing to kill the Jews soon. For the last six days? So, where are the British? To this question, they respond from Jerusalem that all is well.

August 29…

Here is the story as it was recounted to me in the streets of the Safed ghetto, with its mountain air.

"Excuse me, sir, I am the son of the vice-consul of Persia…"

"Of course," I said to the young man. "They did a good job on your house."

"I was on holiday visiting my parents. I am studying in Syria, with the French monks of Antoura.* Ten days ago, the Arabs…"

"I know. Then?"

"Then, on the twenty-ninth, we were all together at home. We hear knocking. My father goes to look out the window. He sees fifty Arabs. 'What do you want, my friends?' he asks them.

"'Come down! We want to kill you with your family.'

"My father knows nearly all of them. 'What? You are my neighbors; I see many of my friends in your group. For twenty years we have shaken hands. My children played with your children.'

"'Today we have to kill you!'

"My father shuts the window and, trusting the robustness of our door, withdraws with my mother, my two sisters, my little brother and me to a room on the first floor.

"Soon, blows of axes against the door. Then the sound of grinding: the door has given way. My father cries out, 'Don't move! I am going to speak to them again.' He goes down. At the foot of the

---

*   Antoura, Lebanon, is the site since 1834 of a French Catholic high school, the Collège Saint Joseph, which still exists today. The young man refers to Syria because Lebanon was at the time grouped together with Syria under the French Mandate for Syria and the Lebanon (1923–1946).

stairs, heading the invasion, is an Arab, his friend. My father holds out his arms and moves toward him to kiss him, saying, 'You, at least, will not do me harm, nor to my family.' The Arab draws a knife from his belt and, with one swoop, slashes my father's head. I was following behind – I couldn't restrain myself. I broke a chair over the head of our friend.

"My father collapsed. The Arab bent down and stabbed him eleven times with his dagger. Afterwards, he looked at him, took him for dead and left to join the others who were pillaging in the adjoining room."

"And then?"

"After pillaging, they set the house on fire. I got my mother, my sisters and my little brother out of the cupboard where they had taken refuge. We were about to drag my father from the fire, when the raging bulls returned. Seeing the blood on the stairs, they said, 'The others slit his throat, let's find his body.'

"I turned to my elder sister and shouted in Arabic, 'Hand me my revolver, Ada!' It was a trick. We had no revolver. My sister pretended to fetch it. The Arabs took fright and left."

Here an old man is blubbering into his white beard. He tells me that his name is Solomon Youa Goldschweig, that he is seventy-two years old, that he was born in Safed, that he never harmed a soul, that they came to his house, that they killed his wife, that they tried to kill him and that it was four of his neighbors, whom he knew well, who did this. He asks me, "Why?"

A young man comes forward. He is Habib David Apriat. His father was a teacher of Hebrew, French and Arabic. Three of his father's former pupils entered his house, killed his father, killed his mother, and cut off the fingers of his sister who pretended to be dead as she lay over her mother.

David Apriat runs off. Where is he going? He returns with his sister – minus two fingers – and the two of them look at me, while the young man keeps repeating, "See! See!"

Another man appears.

"My name is Abraham Levy," he begins. "I am a French citizen, an Algerian. I am the guard at the Alliance Israélite School. I saw everything. When they came into the school, they said, 'Abraham is one of our friends. Don't kill him, just cut off his hands.' I fled to the roof. 'Abraham,' they shouted, 'where are you? You are our friend, we only want to cut off one of your hands!'

"I knew them all. They were all good friends. I managed to get away."

And Chief Rabbi Ismael Cohen?

Three months ago, when I was walking in the Safed ghetto, I visited the old man. He had not set foot on the steep steps of his stone home for over ten years. Eighty-four years old, a proud head, a renowned Talmud scholar.

They slit his throat, too!

I followed the path to his house. I climbed the steps. The door was no longer closed. On the sofa, where he had sat and welcomed me not long ago, lay bloody remnants of clothing. A pool of dry blood stained the tiled floor, like a broken mirror lying on its back. On the wall, the imprints of his bloodstained hands.

"Chief Rabbi," I had said to him in this very place, "please permit my friend Rouquayrol to sketch you."

"Dear visitors," he had replied, "the law of Moses prohibits it, but Ismael Cohen no longer sees well, so he will certainly not notice!"

And he extended his white hand to us.

His hand is there, today, on the wall – all red.

This is what is called a national movement!

CHAPTER 25

See You Soon!

What do the Arabs have to say?

This morning, ten of them gathered together in Jaffa. Five Muslim Arabs: Sheikh Monafar; Omar Bihar, president of the Islamic-Christian Committee; Mahmud Abu Khadra, former governor of Jaffa and mayor of Gaza; Hilini Abu Khadra; and Ismail Nashashibi. Three Catholic Arabs: Nasri Thalamas, Nicolas Beruti and Edmond Roch. And two Greek Orthodox Arabs: I. S. Elissa and Anton Malak.

Once counted, one of them, Edmond Roch, took a car, drove to Tel Aviv and stood on the steps of the Palatin Hotel. He had come to fetch me.

I followed him.

We crossed Tel Aviv rather nervously, holding fast to the wheel. The car stopped on Jaffa's main road. We got out. With Edmond Roch leading the way, we climbed a staircase, found ourselves in front of a door and pushed it open. A large room. The Arabs are there. The atmosphere is charged. Handshaking, eye contact. Eleven chairs. We sit down.

They have so much to say that the large room, which is bare except for the chairs, appears cluttered with their claims. The ten resemble locomotives ready to take off at a hundred miles an hour. Close all level crossings! Let's follow the train!

All of them turn toward Sheikh Monafar.

As a sign of his revered position, the sheikh sports on his head a tarbush swathed with a white ribbon. The sheikh has the tanned skin of desert men. He takes the floor and gets straight to the point: "The land of Palestine is an Arab country; the Arabs were in this country for many years before the Jews."

The other nine murmur in support.

"The Jews, in the course of history, accidentally occupied a few corners of Palestine but never all of it! And during their reign, what did they create? They left nothing in the form of civilization. And what signs remain of their rule? A mosaic! The Romans drove them away. They left. And no trace of them remained. That's about it for the ancient past.

"Five hundred sixty years later, Islam triumphed. Our ancestors retook the land and returned it to its ancient nationality.

"Since then, we have lived in our own home."

"Occupied by the Turks?" I interject.

"Well, we were as though among our own. Until the Great War. During the war, nations woke up, the Arabs like the others. We asked for our ancient kingdom to be reborn and we received promises from England, from France."

"Many times," notes one of the ten.

"Under the Turks…"

No doubt noticing my smile, he replied: "Under the Turks, we had a tough time but we had representatives in Parliament, ministers in the cabinet of Constantinople. And we never ceased demanding greater freedom.

"The official language was Arabic.

"But despite the religious connection which united us with the Turks, our love of freedom pushed us to oppose them. We joined the side of the Allies in the hope of achieving complete independence.

"The Allies won the battle. We shed our blood in this battle. The great Arab kingdom seemed at hand. Then, suddenly it all vanished. We were left with just a dream.

"In the past we were one: Syria, Palestine, Mesopotamia…"

"That's another question," I point out.

"True. We are seven hundred thousand here, right? One can say, I believe, that we represent a national home. But in recompense, Lord Balfour sends us the Jews to build a national home here as well. A national home in another national home – that's war!"

The gathering agrees noisily.

"So you don't want the Jews?" I ask.

"Not true! We do not want a Jewish national home. You know that there are three species of Jews in Palestine. Old religious Jews who come to die here—"

"And you helped them!"

"It was not us who began the massacres! Not us!" exclaim the ten Arabs. "The first person who was killed in this round was an Arab – Sidi Akashe – whose throat was slit in the Sheikh Zorah neighborhood, in Jerusalem, by a Jew."

"On what date?"

They search and come up with August 26. The conflict began on the twenty-third. Had they perhaps gotten the date wrong? Calm is reestablished.

Sheikh Monafar continues: "Then, there are the Jews from before 1919, the baron's Jews. They bought land, they engaged in agriculture, not politics. Then came Lord Balfour's Jews, the Zionists. We have nothing against pious Jews nor against the baron's Jews, they can live in peace here." (People of the Orient! You have forgotten that it was the pious Jews whom you massacred!) "But with the others, we have declared war."

"Of what do you reproach them?"

Again, their voices rise in unison: "Of being a bunch of Europe's castoffs! Of wanting to drive us away! Of treating us like natives! Come on! Does the world not know that there are seven hundred thousand Arabs here? If you want to do what you did in America, go ahead, kill us like you killed the Indians and settle our land! We accuse England! We accuse France!"

"Give me facts!"

"Firstly, we accuse the Jews of ruining us. For example: after lavish overspending, the Tel Aviv Municipality had a debt of one hundred five thousand pounds. The Palestine government paid the debt with treasury money funded by our taxes. Another example: Palestine is a construction site. It has become unrecognizable. We see no need whatsoever for this transformation. Who needs electricity? Who needs all these roads? They are building roads in order to feed Jewish workers. Jewish workers work eight hours, Arab workers twelve hours. Jewish workers are paid twice as much as Arab workers. The government that we subsidize is not a government but a charitable organization for foreigners.

"Secondly, we accuse them of scheming against us. The laws of the country were made by an Englishman, a Jew, Mr. Bentwich.* The laws favor the Jews, not the Arabs. For the same violation: a two-pound fine for a Jew and two months in jail for an Arab.

"Thirdly, we accuse them of driving us out of our home. The country is called Palestine – they call it Eretz Yisrael [the Land of Israel]! The only language used to be Arabic, now they have succeeded in putting Hebrew on an equal footing. They buy our best

---

*   Norman Bentwich (1883–1971), attorney general of Mandate Palestine.

lands." (Why do you sell them?) "They say: 'If you are unhappy, take the bones of your prophets and leave!'"

So, in the place of the Wandering Jew, we have the wandering Arab?

"Sirs, what terms are you demanding in order to stop massacring the Jews?"

Uproar! They never massacred Jews! Never! Or rather, if I understood correctly, they did not massacre them in order to massacre them but only to draw attention to the fate of the Arabs.

"Our terms," said the Sheikh, "are thus: (1) annulment of the Balfour Declaration as it stands and as it is applied; (2) elections based on universal suffrage and formation of an Arab government; (3) limits on Jewish immigration; (4) annulment of laws favoring Jews and their industries."

"Do you believe that the fifty-two countries that ratified the Balfour Declaration can go back on their word?"

"It is not our business!"

Indeed, in terms of nations, they seem only interested in the fifty-third and the fifty-fourth: the Arab nation and the Jewish nation!

"Sirs, I met your two leaders in Jerusalem: the grand mufti and Ragheb Bey al-Nashashibi. I asked the grand mufti, 'Are the massacres going to end?' The grand mufti, who is young but not foolhardy, clapped his hands. We were sitting on his terrace. The Mosque of Omar served as a backdrop and darkness engulfed the Mount of Olives. Everything seemed peaceful around us. At his call, servants came running. The descendant of the prophet asked for paper. I lent him a pencil. He answered me in writing. Here is the document."

I read it out: "'One cannot hope for a real and continued improvement in Palestine, for permanent security, general calm, good relations between the inhabitants of the country, unless (1) the unjust policy, contained in the Balfour Declaration, contrary to the nature of things and requiring the subservience of the majority to the minority, is annulled; (2) a regime of justice and equity is adopted. This regime consists in the formation of a democratic representative state ruled by all the Palestinians, Arabs and Jews, in proportion to their respective numbers.'

"Do you agree with the grand mufti?"

"Yes!"

"Then, gentlemen, I left the Old City. What silence! What shivers down my spine! 'Careful!' I shouted, each time a shadow emerged. 'Do not disembowel me! I come from Paris, not from Tel Aviv.' I reached the town hall. Ragheb Bey al-Nashashibi received me. Ragheb Bey, who is a valiant man, gazed at me with even more frankness in his eyes than three months ago.

"'Well, honorable mayor,' I said. 'Did you get your payment? At the price of blood, you told me last May. Well, the blood has been shed!'

"Ragheb Bey looked at me surprised. He said that as long as the Balfour Declaration stood, nothing had ended. As soon as the English troops departed, it would all begin again.

"Do you agree with the mayor of Jerusalem?"

"Yes!"

"'Look,' I told your leader, 'you can't kill all the Jews. They number one hundred fifty thousand. It would take too long!'

"'No,' he said in a very soft voice. 'Just two days!'

"'Seventy-five thousand per day?'

"'No problem!'"

I asked the ten if they agreed with Ragheb Bey.

"Definitely!"

"So, gentlemen, when the English troops board their ships, do me a favor and send me a telegram. I think that you are overestimating your strength. The new Jews are not going to let themselves bleed to death. I am even certain that they will pay you back in kind. It will be a tough battle. Here is my address. Don't forget to notify me.

"I shall return to watch you at work. See you soon!"

CHAPTER 26

The Joy of Being Jewish

I scoured Judea, Samaria, Upper and Lower Galilee. In vain, I climbed Mount Carmel, Mount Tabor and Mount Gilboa; in vain I cried out in the Jezreel Valley; in vain I rowed on the Sea of Galilee. "Show me one Jew," I cried to the assembled, "just one who hails from France. I am not asking for two; a very small one will do!" My calls remained unanswered. No Jew had arrived from France to reconstruct the kingdom of David.

England has one. He possesses a beautiful soul which illuminates his handsome face. Above his desk in Jerusalem hangs a signed portrait of Marshal Foch.* This Englishman was a colonel in the English army. But one day he became aware of his Jewishness. He gave up his stripes and his nationality and arrived bare in the city of his forefathers. Now his fervor illuminates the dome of the Zionist temple like an eternal candle. He is still called Colonel Kisch.†

---

* Marshal Ferdinand Jean Marie Foch (1851–1929), French general who commanded the Allied troops at the end of World War I.

† Frederick Hermann Kisch (1888–1943), lieutenant colonel in the British army (later promoted to brigadier as the highest-ranking Jewish officer in the British armed forces) and committed Zionist. He would later be killed fighting in World War II.

Holland also has one: a magistrate from Amsterdam. His name is Van Vriesland.[*] He is in charge of the consulate of his native country in Palestine. He is a man of the world who loves cigars but also upholds the idea that the flowers, in the garden of humanity, should strive to maintain their colors. He does not think it useful that a flower, on the pretext of assimilating, should resemble another flower. He believes it is right for a Jew to dream of sitting again under his own fig tree.

Czechoslovakia sent teachers; Belgium, planters; Germany, architects; America, rich amateurs. If you were, for one moment, to set up a barrier on Herzl Street in Tel Aviv, you would find one hundred men, each with a wonderful story. This one, for being a Jew, crossed Russia, Siberia, Manchuria and China – on foot! He left like a rocket, without bothering to take the shortest route. Others came from Canada, from Chile.

The smell of the Promised Land does not only lure the barefoot. Look at those gentlemen roaming across the country, their souls on fire; they are millionaires. One comes from Poland: he is a big manufacturer from Lodz who has twelve thousand workers under him; his name is Oscar Kohn.[†] See how inspired he is. He came for fifteen days: now he does not want to leave. He is looking for water and is determined to find it. Then he will set up his mills here. This powerful industrialist has become intoxicated with the Jewish poem – what a strange fable! Other magnates, the Polak brothers from Moscow, heard the same song; they are milling flour to the tune of idealism!

---

[*]   Siegfried Adolf Van Vriesland (1886–1939), Dutch attorney. He was treasurer of the World Zionist Executive (1919–1925) and later became general manager of the Port of Tel Aviv.

[†]   Oscar Kohn was a successful textile manufacturer in Lodz. He arrived in Palestine after his son was killed in Poland in February 1929.

Painters, men of letters, musicians, actors… But the bulk of the herd hail from Lithuania, Ukraine, Bessarabia, Bukovina and Galicia.

Are they happy? How do they live? Tell us their customs, you say.

Yes, they are happy. One might think that it costs me little to make such a statement. But I spent time in Palestine. I saw Jews plowing the land. As I passed, I cried out, "Shalom!" and peered into their homes. Seeing that everyone had a bed on which they could lie at night, I said to myself, "Good, good!" I saw their stacks of wheat and that their communally raised children were magnificent children. I saw how these astonishing farmers returned home, at night, from torrid fields, and proceeded to open bookcases. The books they read are the books of intellectuals. I also saw women toiling the land, backs bent – then they stood up, came toward you, and suddenly they were *ladies* who were walking. I wiped my forehead, bid them shalom again and departed, leaving them in the harsh plains. Is that happiness?

Three months later, I returned. I visited again the Jezreel Valley, Tiberias, Haifa. Nothing had changed. They ploughed the land like peasants plough the land, without fuss.

"So!" I said to them. "Did the Arabs attack you?"

"Yes."

"You refused to give in to them?"

"Right."

And, far from the lands where they were born, they resumed thrashing wheat, their rifles at their sides. Is this happiness?

I saw them in Jerusalem, in the neighborhoods they have constructed. Because of them, their ancient brothers had closed their stores inside the walls. You no longer saw them scurrying through the labyrinths. The Wall no longer wailed. No more silk robes, no more marvelous hats. The pious Jews have vanished! But Theodor

Herzl's young musketeers were on the watch. What was that rumor? Who was going to be assassinated tonight? The chauffeur was reluctant to drive on the main road. That building dominating the Mount of Olives, on the left, is the British High Commission. All its employees are on the side of the Arabs. Was this encouraging? Was it possible, at least, to make a fortune in this country? No way! Was this happiness?

But, here, it is brighter, more welcoming. Here, life is tangible: Tel Aviv! They say that the traders are in financial straits. But the faces show no sign of distress. Tonight, the entire – entire – city is returning home from a soccer game won by the Maccabeans.* Forty thousand people are in the street, as though to demonstrate what the Arabs will be in for on the set date of the great massacre. Is this happiness?

Mr. Dizengoff, you built Tel Aviv and cast Theodor Herzl's dream in cement. But while you are showing us the plans that will turn Tel Aviv into a capital of one hundred thousand inhabitants, we can hear knocks at the door of the city: your neighbors, the Muslims, are warning you that soon they will demolish your work. Are you happy?

Mr. Rutenberg,† you brought light to the city of your forefathers. In Russia, where you were a big shot, you would have been feted for having dispelled the darkness. Here, the Arabs accuse you of stealing their water. The Christians thumb their noses at the man who dared to touch the Jordan River. You would be well advised to surround your bold enterprise with barbed wire. Are you happy?

---

*   Reference to the Maccabi soccer club, founded in 1906.

†   Pinhas Rutenberg (1879–1942), founder of the Palestine Electric Company and supporter of other important institutions in Mandate Palestine, including the Haganah (precursor to the Israel Defense Forces, Israel's modern army).

Mr. Tolkowski,* you used to be Belgian. Misery did not bring you to Palestine. You had a good life. In 1921, during the first pogroms in Jaffa, you lost someone dear to you. Recently, you were in Talpiot† when the Arabs attacked. You counted your bullets: one for your wife, three for your children, one for a relative, and one for yourself. You had nine bullets in all; that left you with three to defend yourself. You made your decision. Simultaneously, at the exit from Tel Aviv, the Arabs were murdering your brother-in-law, young Goldberg, who had come to the rescue of two Jews stranded in an orange grove. When I saw you again, you were rather pale but had no regrets being a Palestinian citizen. Are you happy?

And you, over there, in the fields – Lithuanians, Ukrainians, Bessarabians, Bukovinans and Galicians – why would you be nostalgic? Working the soil in the plain of Esdraelon‡ is certainly not the height of happiness: it is hot, the flies are voracious and there is no chance of striking it rich, but then where did you come from? Were you happier under the yoke of the Europeans?

Is a square in Tel Aviv less good for business than the squares of New York, London, Constantinople or Paris? What a discovery! Was the square of Lwow any better? Or that of Kovno? Did you all do good business in Berdichev? Zhitomir? Tarnopol? Kishinev? You are as poor here as you were there? Perhaps! But what are the Jews trying to find in Palestine? A fortune? No, a country!

Of this, there can be no doubt. These are Jews who have the Jewish homeland in their blood. What one calls "Zionism" is nothing more than an illness of the soul of Israel. This illness does not

---

* Shemuel Tolkowsky (1886–1965), Zionist diplomat, businessman and public servant. He moved to Mandate Palestine in 1911.

† A Jerusalem neighborhood.

‡ An alternate name for the Jezreel Valley.

affect all Jews, but those who have been bitten are truly under its spell. One does not become a Zionist by reason; Zionism is, I believe, the opposite of reason. One is a Zionist by instinct. It is a passion and, every day, one encounters masses of people who cannot resist this passion.

A man who actualizes his passion is a happy man.

Colonel Kisch, Consul Van Vriesland, Mayor Dizengoff, engineer Rutenberg, planter Tolkowski, the extremist Jabotinsky who foresees four million Jews in thirty years' time on the land of his forefathers,* Czechoslovakian librarians, German doctors, Hebrew poets, farm girls with white hands, visionary drivers, pretty students from America, young couples who make "*mizmuz*" on street corners. *Mizmuz!* That's how they say the word *flirt* in Hebrew! Flirting in Hebrew! The rabbis' diatribes against these young Jews are clearly not always groundless! The plowmen, customer-less traders, dreamers and tough guys – they have gotten what they wanted. Zionists, they live in Zion. The bad returned home and only the pure remained.

Are they happy? Profoundly happy to be Jewish. Elsewhere, anywhere in the rest of the world, when a Jew does something bad, he is no longer a Frenchman, or a German, or a Belgian or an Englishman – he is a Jew! And when a Jew discovers something important and brings honor to mankind, he is no longer a Jew but

---

*   The Jewish population of what is today the State of Israel did not reach four million on Jabotinsky's timetable (by 1960), but it did surpass four million some time in the early 1990s. Today it is approximately six million, with an additional two million non-Jews for a total population of around eight million. Itamar Rabinovich and Jehuda Reinharz, eds., *Israel in the Middle East: Documents and Readings on Society, Politics, and Foreign Relations, Pre-1948 to the Present* (Waltham, MA: Brandeis University Press, 2008), 571–72.

a German, a Belgian, an Englishman or a Frenchman. In the eyes of everyone, Einstein is a German, and Bergson is a Frenchman. All the Jews here say that they had enough of contributing to the enrichment of English, Russian, French, German and American culture. In Palestine, their pride is satisfied. They have won the right to be villains or geniuses without ceasing to be Jews.

Life in Paris and London? It is certainly more beautiful than life in Palestine. But is it more beautiful than their dream?

And the massacres? Yes, they would have represented a major challenge for a people used to peace. But for them…

When, on the first night, Adam saw the sun set, he cried. The day had been so beautiful! But on the next day, the sun reappeared and joy returned to the heart of the first man. And when the sun disappeared again, he sang. Adam understood that this is how it would always be. He stopped despairing and said, "Let us live!"

Live, then, Jews! From massacre to massacre…

CHAPTER 27

Wandering Jew,
Have You Arrived?

Wandering Jew, have you arrived? When I met him, this winter, as he made his way across the Carpathians, I truly thought that he was walking to Palestine. The sun was rising for him, once again, over the land of Canaan. According to Zephaniah, son of Cushi, of Gedaliah, of Amariah and of Hezekiah, Zion sang songs, Israel shouted cries of happiness and Jerusalem exulted with joy. Having driven away its enemies, the Lord had, at last, annulled His punitive decree. I heard everywhere, in the chancelleries of Europe and of America, that England, obeying the word of God, was going to bring back the exiled one and make his name famous in the land where he had suffered opprobrium.

I was happy for him.

If the world consisted solely of France or America, Germany or England, Zionism would not exist. The voice of the prophets of return would be talking solely to the deaf. Could Nehemiah have come to Paris, London, Berlin or New York and said, "Go to Judah, to the city of thy fathers' graves, so that you may rebuild it"?

The graves of the fathers now lie in Pere-Lachaise.* In these prosaic times, Zionism, seen from the stock-exchange square, seems like a prankster's joke. That is Paris-Israel talking. Its view is not mine. The "ideal," I know, is not always profitable. Nor do we eat the flowers we put on the table.

But let us respect the facts. The Jews of the Atlantic have ceased being Jews of Zion. One could proffer a host of academic reasons as to why their souls do not sing to the bow of Theodor Herzl. Suffice it to say that being Jewish does not mean one is a poet. Under Godfrey of Bouillon, all Christians were not crusaders. French Jews who look at Palestine do so from afar and from the end of a very powerful telescope.

Let us, therefore, situate the Jewish question where it truly lies: in Poland, Russia, Romania, Czechoslovakia and Hungary. That's where the Wandering Jew wanders. A Jew from these countries is to other men what a mad dog from the African backwoods is to other dogs. He roams, searching for food. If he tries to get close to a town, the townspeople point their rifles at him. Let us leave our frontiers a little. The world is not contained within the map of France. A drama is taking place in our time: an ancient, suddenly revived drama, a poignant drama: the drama of the Jewish race.

In Russia, the Jews are waiting to be massacred. The day the Soviets retreat, the Red Cross can prepare their ambulances. The Aryan pack will bare its fangs.

The butt of hatred in Poland, the butt of hatred in Romania. A thick layer of hatred covers them like stone, in perpetuity! In the Marmarosh Mountains, they lie at the bottom of the great Carpathian pit, unable to scratch their way back up. Brute misery!

It is there, in these countries, that a magic lantern projected a vision of the Promised Land. A new Promised Land – not the

---

* A cemetery in Paris.

ancient, grey-hued one of Moses, but a new, modern Promised Land, in color, in the color of the Union Jack! The Wandering Jew stopped in his tracks. It was so beautiful, the country that was depicted to him. Sun! Oranges? Trees with which to build his house!

"Truly," he cried, like Sanballat in the reign of Artaxerxes,* "what are you doing, wretched Jews? Do you seriously intend to rebuild Jerusalem? Will you be able to transform these piles of dust into the stones that were burned?"

"You bet," answered a white-haired Englishman.

"Are you Artaxerxes, known as Long-Hand?" asked the Wandering Jew.

"In our times," answered the white-haired man, "it is no longer the hand but the arm that needs to be long. I am Balfour, known as Long-Arm."

Then the Wandering Jew said to the Lord: "If it seems good to the Lord and if Your servant has found favor in his eyes, send me to Judah."

"Here are letters, my good Jew," answered the lord, "letters for the governors of the lands that lie beyond the rivers and the mountains, letters that will enable you to pass through these lands and arrive at the country of my magic lantern."

And following the long arm of the English lord, the Wandering Jew reached the land of Palestine ten years ago.

***

He soon noticed that more than one hundred thousand others had followed him. So he said to them, "Let us rise up and build."†

But enemies lay all around them, watchful.

---

*   Sanballat was a Samarian leader who opposed the rebuilding of Jerusalem by Nehemiah, as decreed by Artaxerxes I of Persia in 444 BCE.

†   Nehemiah 2:18.

You will understand right away that these were the Arabs. There were Arabs in the shadow of Lord Balfour's long arm. "So what!" said those who arrived from Galicia, Ukraine, Bessarabia, Bukovina. "We shall work with one hand and brandish a sword with the other, just as our forefathers did when they returned, like us, in the spring of 537 before Jesus Christ."*

And they did as they said.

They bought one hundred thirteen thousand hectares† of land. They founded one hundred one settlements. Since they did not have to rebuild the walls of Jerusalem, which had not been destroyed after they were last rebuilt, or place doors, locks and bars on the gates, they built impressive neighborhoods on the doorstep of the holy city. Dizengoff built Spring Hill (Tel Aviv). Rutenberg married the Jordan to the Yarmuk. Tolkowski planted orange groves.

What wonderful history! But Wandering Jew, where did you find the money?

All over the world.

When your dispersed brothers saw you resolutely take up your cane and march straight from the Carpathians to the Jordan, their eyes were fixed upon you. You were a national hero to them. Just for you, every day, at any hour and on any pretext, marks, dollars, shillings, pesos and florins were dropped into the little blue collection boxes with the Shield of David that had been distributed in every land where your fellow men live.

This is when you began to do stupid things.

---

*	Approximate date when the Jews returned to Jerusalem after their exile in Babylon.

†	An area of 279,000 acres, just a little smaller than the total area of the city of Los Angeles, California.

Your old wanderer's stick became haughty like a halberd.* You let it drop coldly on the feet of the Arabs; your restless, impassioned spirit brushed aside twenty centuries with a flip of the mind. You returned home, like the nobles who followed Louis XVIII,† without wishing to know who, since your departure, had bought your house. Insolence is not always a bad thing, but it should at least be aimed at those who hold power!

You had enough of living under a boot. Everyone can understand how good it must feel to raise your head up high. But if you go around with your head in the air, you cannot see what is happening around you. Wandering Jew, the English lord has withdrawn his arm!

You, with your clean-shaven face, cropped hair, caftan abandoned in the garbage, liberated neck in its open collar, you strutted proudly above the common folk!

Don't deny it. I saw you. You marched behind a flag, like a soccer captain, shoulders high like a fireman! When one has inspired pity for so long, it is tempting to want to inspire respect. But when you shed your skin, my friend, you should not do so on your balcony, otherwise you may catch a nasty illness.

But you stood there, leaning on the railings, shouting your secrets to every passerby. General-in-chief, you distributed your battle plans within the enemy camp. This year, you will collect one million pounds more than last year and you will buy Mount Carmel! "Listen, Arabs," you said. "You want to know my goal? This is it: it is the creation, here, of a Jewish majority. Do you know what I am doing in Zurich this year? Ensuring for myself no more, no

---

*   An axe mounted on a spear, a weapon used in the fifteenth and sixteenth centuries.

†   Louis XVIII returned from exile in 1814 to restore the French monarchy after the French Revolution and Napoleonic era.

less, than all of Palestine. The Jewish Agency, dear Arabs, which the congress[*] has just created, will enable me to persuade non-wandering Jews to buy this beautiful land. In ten years, it will be mine. In twenty years, five hundred thousand of my little brothers will come join me. The white-haired lord, known as Long-Arm, will elevate me to the ranks of Canada and of Australia. I will become the sixth dominion. Hurrah!"

And then you played "Hatikvah"!

What did your neighbor, the dear Arab, do?

He first looked all around. Ah! The long-armed lord has gone! Then, he started to count. You were not yet five hundred thousand – this was the moment to act. He drew close, on tiptoe, and, while you were vaunting your glory, he clobbered you right in the neck.

Wandering Jew, how are you faring?

Well, he is not doing too badly. One would expect to find him in a poorer condition, following the bleeding. His skin is a little pale, his voice less firm, his gait somewhat wobbly, but he is not bedridden. Above all – and this is the sensational new fact in the entire life of the Wandering Jew – he has not bowed his head!

***

After all these events, I found myself on the beach in Tel Aviv. It was the first day of the Jewish year: Rosh Hashanah. At the edge of the water, the Jews were acting very strangely. They seemed to be delving into their pockets in order to find something to throw. Then, they extended their arms in the direction of the Mediterranean: they were casting their sins into the sea![†]

---

[*]   Reference to the Sixteenth Zionist Congress, held in Zurich in 1929.

[†]   On the festival of Rosh Hashanah, it is customary to symbolically cast off one's sins into a flowing body of water. The ceremony is known as Tashlich.

"It is about time!" I said to myself. "They have finally understood. As long as they do not forget to drown their excess pride, everything will end well."

Is this a prophecy?

Has the Wandering Jew arrived?

Why not?

About the Author

For Londres, humanity was always divided into two cate-
gories: those who possessed furniture and those who possessed a suitcase.

Pierre Assouline, *Albert Londres: Vie et mort d'un grand
reporter, 1884–1932* (Albert Londres: Life and death of
an international reporter, 1884–1932)

Albert Londres was born in Vichy in 1884 and grew up in a
simple working-class family. His unusual surname is believed
to derive from the Spanish Loundrès, which became Gallicized over
time to Londres. At the age of seventeen, in light of his poor showing at school, Londres was sent by his parents to train as a bookkeeper in Lyon. But the bourgeois life was clearly not suited to a
young man who burned with a love of poetry and the arts. In 1903,
Londres abandoned his training to try his luck in Paris.

He arrived in the capital without a dime and proceeded to live a
typical bohemian life in a sparse Montmartre garret with his childhood sweetheart, Marcelle Laforest. In 1904, their daughter Florise
was born. Tragically, a year later Marcelle fell sick from starvation
and died. Heartbroken, Londres poured his feelings into verse,

publishing his first volume of poetry. He went on to publish three more, the last in 1910. Little Florise was raised by her paternal grandparents but Londres remained close to her throughout his life.

After working briefly for the Paris branch of *Le Salut Public*, a Lyon newspaper, Londres landed his first major job in 1906, as parliamentary reporter for *Le Matin*. With the outbreak of WWI in 1914, he was sent, as a war correspondent, to cover the hostilities on the Belgian front and gained renown with the publication of his first major article, on the bombing of Reims Cathedral. A fellow journalist described his writing as a blend of reporting, poetry and a page of history.

Dissatisfied with covering just the home front, Londres aspired to greater things. He wanted to go to the Dardanelles, where the momentous Battle of Gallipoli was unfolding, but his boss refused his request. Londres threatened to quit and when told "OK, go!" he crossed the road and found a job with *Le Petit Journal*, a rival paper that promptly dispatched him to the Dardanelles.

After the war, he traveled to Spain to cover the volatile political situation there. His reports from the Iberian Peninsula already displayed the succinct metaphoric style that was to make his writing so distinctive. "Two illnesses plague the country. One is known but has not yet found a doctor. It is Catalonia. The other is surfacing: Andalusia. Catalonia wants freedom. Andalusia bread. The central government is caught between the two sides. It is pulmonary congestion."* Londres was one of the first journalists to predict an escalation of events in Spain as a result of a new "microbe" called Bolshevism.

In 1919 he joined the illustrated daily *Excelsior*, which sent him to Lebanon and Syria, where he witnessed the birth of Arab

---

*   *Le Petit Journal*, January 24, 1919, cited in Assouline, *Albert Londres*, 159.

nationalism. Commenting on the rebel tribes, he wrote: "They prefer to be masters over a ruin than citizens in the midst of a happy people. They call this a cry for independence."* He mocked Syria's pretense at national unity, in view of the dozens of ethnicities that populated the region.

In 1920, when every entry door was tightly closed to journalists, Londres succeeded in penetrating the Soviet Union. To do so he needed to knock on endless doors, shuttle between cities and obtain a mountain of permits. After acquiring his eighteenth visa, he arrived in Petrograd. He described two predominant moods: fear and hunger. He saw desperately empty storefronts and seven hundred thousand citizens with only one idea in mind: to eat. He found the same scenes on the streets of Moscow and concluded that the Soviets had devised a new form of absolute monarchy for the twentieth century, with a king called His Majesty Proletariat the First.[†]

In Bulgaria, he interviewed the young monarch Boris II. In Switzerland he chased after exiled Charles IV, the last Austro-Hungarian emperor, laying siege at his hotel till he obtained an interview. In 1922 he reported from India, where he met Mahatma Gandhi and Rabindranath Tagore. In Calcutta he shocked the aristocratic British guests by inviting a "native" to dine at his table in the luxurious Great Eastern Hotel.

In 1923, after a brief spell with the new daily *Le Quotidien*, Londres joined the staff of *Le Petit Parisien*, where he would do his finest reporting. The year marked a turning point in his life as a journalist. No longer a mere reporter, he became a righter of wrongs, an investigative reporter par excellence. His reports on France's penal colonies, specifically in Cayenne, French Guiana, made him

---

*   *Excelsior*, December 29, 1919, cited in Assouline, *Albert Londres*, 181.

†   Cited in Assouline, *Albert Londres*, 203.

a national hero and played no small part in leading to the abolition of these colonies in 1937. As Londres's biographer, Pierre Assouline, notes: "Henceforth Londres was convinced that his reports were not simply historical testimonies, at best, but catalysts that helped make men suffer less."* After each series, Londres collated his articles and published them in book form.

In 1924, he set out for North Africa to file a series of exposés on France's repressive military penitentiaries. Back home, he covered the Tour de France, which he dubbed the "tour of suffering." In 1925, he decided to investigate lunatic asylums, infiltrating his way into closed institutions in the guise of a dentist, guard, family member and even madman. The same year took him back to the Middle East to cover the Druze revolt in Syria. In 1926 he reported from Poland on the military coup that brought Józef Piłsudski back to power. In 1927, Argentina and the white slave trade. In 1928, Africa and the "black slave trade," which caused the deaths of thousands of exploited African workers.

In 1929, he traveled to London, Prague, Subcarpathia, Poland and Palestine for a series of twenty-seven articles on the lives of Jews. He subsequently published the articles in book form under the title *The Wandering Jew Has Arrived.*

In 1930, he reported on the pearl fishers of the Persian Gulf. In 1931, he followed the tracks of Macedonian revolutionaries in Bulgaria. He then decided to go on a secret mission to China. His boss at *Le Petit Parisien* balked at the idea. Londres resigned and was immediately offered better terms and the green light at another French daily, *Le Journal.* In December 1931, he set off, revealing to no one, not even his bosses, the purpose of his mission. Drug trafficking, arms dealing and Bolshevik meddling in Chinese affairs

---

*   Ibid., 355.

have all been cited as possible targets of his investigation. In January 1932, being on the spot in Shanghai, Londres was able to report on the Sino-Japanese hostilities. He then disappeared for a month. When he resurfaced in Shanghai, he promised to file an "explosive" investigation on his return to France. In May, he set sail for home aboard the *Georges Philippar* liner.

On the sixteenth, in the middle of the night, fire broke out aboard ship, trapping Londres in his cabin. Unable to swim, he refused to jump into the water. Desperate attempts on the part of the crew to rescue him were of no avail. The intrepid reporter disappeared in the flames at the age of forty-eight.

In 1933, his daughter Florise inaugurated the Albert Londres Prize for best journalist of the year in memory of her father.

As Assouline so accurately writes: "Despite Londres's brief life, he influenced generations of journalists.... He was a rare individual who observed man not from a telescope but from a magnifying glass…with talent, courage and humor."[*]

---

[*]   Ibid., 22.